Law and its Presuppositions

International Library of Philosophy

Editor: Ted Honderich
Professor of Philosophy, University College, London

A catalogue of books already published in the
International Library of Philosophy
will be found at the end of this volume

Law and its Presuppositions

Actions, agents and rules

S.C. Coval

Professor of Philosophy
University of British Columbia

and

J.C. Smith

Professor of Law
University of British Columbia

ROUTLEDGE & KEGAN PAUL
London, Boston and Henley

First published in 1986
by Routledge & Kegan Paul plc

14 Leicester Square, London WC2H 7PH, England

9 Park Street, Boston, Mass. 02108, USA and

Broadway House, Newtown Road,
Henley on Thames, Oxon RG9 1EN, England

Set in Times 10pt
by Columns Ltd of Reading
and printed in Great Britain
by Billing and Sons Ltd,
Worcester

Library of Congress Cataloging in Publication Data
Coval, S.C. (Samuel Charles), 1931-
Law and its presuppositions.
(International library of philosophy)
Bibliography: p.
Includes index.
1. Law – Philosophy. I. Smith, J.C. (Joseph C.)
II. Title. III. Series.
K230.C68L39 1986 340'.1 85-18324
ISBN 0-7102-0446-9

To our parents
Louis Coval
Lillian Coval
Lillian Smith
Reginald Smith

CONTENTS

ACKNOWLEDGMENTS

We would like to acknowledge and express our appreciation for the help and services of the following: Peter Burns, who co-authored 'The concept of action and its juridical significance', from which we drew sections of chapters 1 and 2, and which appeared in the *University of Toronto Law Journal*, 1980, vol. 30; *The Cambridge Law Journal* and *The University of Toronto Law Journal* for agreeing to allow the use of certain materials from articles published there by the authors; Joe Naylor, Jim and Linda Andersen, Dr DeLloyd Guth, Joan Rush, and Dr Rosemary Rosemary Carter; the Social Sciences and Humanities Research Council of Canada for Leave Fellowships which made this work possible.

I

THE CONCEPT OF ACTION

Among the most basic of legal concepts of concern to the practitioners of law at all levels we find those of defence, culpability, negligence, responsibility and obligation. But to wield these concepts requires understanding of another concept – the concept of what it is to do something. Law is about actions. We intend to describe the relevant rudiments of that concept of action which is part of our common understanding. Clearly, this cannot be the final position on such matters but it will tell us where we are. The law, in order to operate as it does, must in an unself-conscious way already work with some concept of action or other. A later project, in Chapter II, will deal with the relations between the assumed or implied legal conception of an action and the conception we argue is part of our common understanding. Once in possession of that concept we shall be in a favourable position to evaluate many of the legal notions which have been derived without benefit of the realization that they must be compatible with the idea of what an act is. We turn now to that matter.

1 ADJUSTERS

There will exist in any natural language or other representation of our understanding of the world a primary set of concepts which classifies favoured phenomena according to a rather stable set of criteria and a secondary set of concepts which classifies the well-known and recurrent aberrations of these favoured cases. Thus we have 'tomatoes' and things which on occasion we can say 'look like tomatoes'[1] but may or may not be; we have 'John's poisoning the pigeons' and 'John's accidentally poisoning the pigeons'.

Standard and adjuster terms are common phenomena in natural language. Two broad classes of adjusters are action adjusters and epistemological adjusters; the first marks well-known and recurrent deviations from a standard in our claims about actions, the second marks well-known and recurrent deviations from a standard among our knowledge claims. Naturally we will be concerned here only with the former.

Consider the following list of action adjusters:

(1) Accidentally
(2) *Mis*takenly
(3) *In*advertently
(4) Care*lessly*
(5) *In*voluntarily
(6) *Un*intentionally

Each action adjuster cancels a feature or set of features of a standard case of action, thus marking an important way in which an action deviates from the standard. Notice that each of these terms except 'accidentally' contains an overt negative, a fact in keeping with its cancelling function. 'Accidentally', however, contains an overt negative in its dictionary definition: 'An act due to an *un*foreseen event, etc.' The attenuated cases of action are worthy of treatment as standard deviants because each marks an important way in which a standard action may fail. Each such well-known aberration, marked by an adjuster term, is retained within the radius of the concept of an action. One of the objects of this chapter will be to explain why that, rather than another, should be our taxonomical policy.

Despite our present conceptual arrangements, each aberration does have a possible description quite independent of its present agreed dependence upon the standard case of an action. Thus, as we shall see, we can give a description of any action adjuster in terms of the abilities of agents.

The following things about these cancellers must be remembered:

(1) They mark standard or typical deviations from a standard.
(2) They are kept within the conceptual ambit of the standard concept for various good policy reasons, which we will discuss later.
(3) They each cancel a set of features of the standard case.
(4) They assert (or imply) specific ways in which the deviations are like the standard case.
(5) They also assert (or imply) specific ways in which the deviations positively differ from the standard case.
(6) They are independently describable (although, as pointed out, we choose to keep them as deviations to a dominant conceptual theme).
(7) Since each adjuster functions by cancellation upon some feature of the standard concept to which it is attached, we can, by conversion, uncover these feature we have affirmatively and originally set into the standard case itself.

We propose to do the following: give an account of each typically deviant case which shows what features of the standard are cancelled; schematize each such deviant case to show what constitutes its deviance affirmatively and apart from the cancellation of features of the standard; show which features the standard case of an action has by converting the cancellations performed by the terms for the deviants; discuss the policy that motivates the concept of an action through its attenuated descriptions; and outline the significance of the theory for the law. Although we think the distinctions among the actions to be described are properly named, nothing important hangs on the propriety of the names. What is important is that these are the *bona fide* independent distinctions which function in the way we describe, however named.

(1) Accidentally

J.L. Austin has set us on the right track with a lucid and now famous example which allows us to readily separate accidents from mistakes:[2] I intend to shoot my donkey which is pastured along with yours in the field behind the house. I have him in my sights preparatory to squeezing the trigger; your donkey suddenly veers and, just as I squeeze off the shot, charges across the fatal line of flight. I have accidentally killed your donkey. It will be useful to schematically diagram this sort of deviation (Figure 1.1).

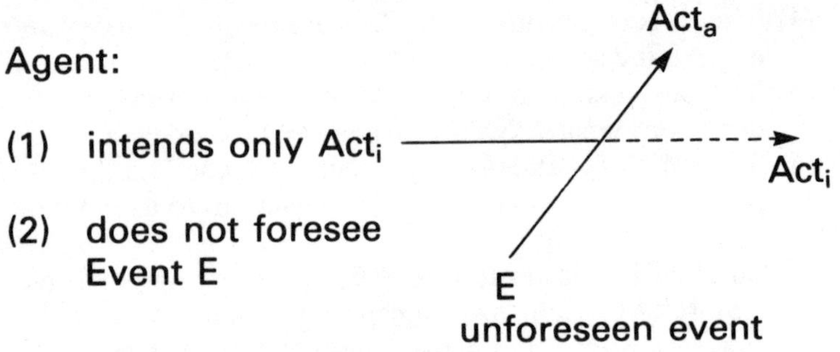

Figure 1.1

To generalize: in cases of accident the agent intends to perform an action, Act_i, which does not succeed because an unforeseen event occurs which produces a vector effect on the agent's behaviour and, consequently, an unintended result: the accidental Act_a.

A classical legal example of an accident is furnished by the facts of *Stanley v. Powell*[3] where a pellet from a gun fired, according to the jury, without negligence (Act_i) glanced off a branch of a tree (the unforeseen event) and struck the plaintiff in the eye (Act_a).

(2) *Mistakenly*

A patient enters a hospital to have an ingrown toe-nail removed. The doctor, believing the patient to be someone else, performs a vasectomy on him.[4] The doctor has mistakenly sterilized the patient.

The generalization of this case is to be easily seen from its schematic representation (Figure 1.2).

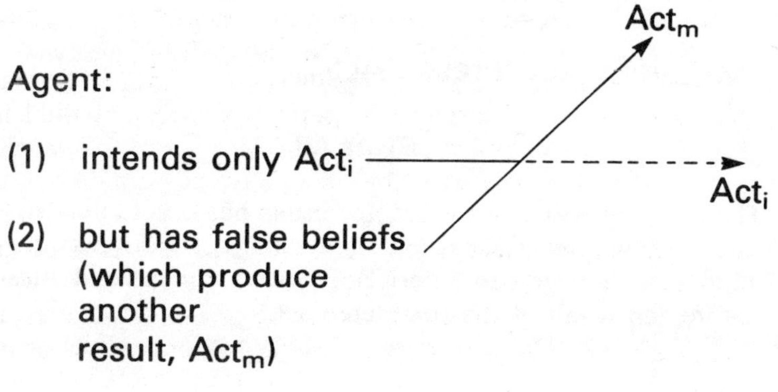

Figure 1.2

Act_i would be the intended sterilization of the other patient and Act_m is the sterilization of the unfortunate one.

(3) Inadvertently

Menlove stacked his hay in his hayrick. The hay spontaneously ignited and burned down Vaughan's cottages.[5] Menlove inadvertently burned the cottages. To say that he burned them unintentionally is true but incomplete since he could have burned them accidentally, mistakenly or carelessly. The absence of intent does not distinguish between these aberrant actions, but it does serve to distinguish them from involuntariness. What then has to be added in order to fill out inadvertence or, to put the question more naturally, what has been cancelled from a standard case of action by the concept of inadvertence? Clearly, intention has been cancelled, but not the intention of the main act. Menlove did intend to stack his hay. But he did not intend nor foresee the *resultant* event. The schematic representation of inadvertence would look as shown in Figure 1.3.

Agent:

(1) intends only $Act_i \longrightarrow Act_i \longrightarrow Act_{inad}$

(2) does not foresee Act_{inad}

Figure 1.3

The agent performs Act_i; $Act_{inad.}$ results but is not intended. We can see now how accident and inadvertence are distinct: the first implies an unforeseen interfering event, the second only an unforeseen result of the completed act.

(4) Carelessly

If in pushing a passenger on to a moving train a guard dislodges a package from under his arm, causing it to fall under the wheels of the train, he could be said to have dislodged the parcel carelessly.[6] Notice that the canceller 'carelessly' makes it clear that the dislodging of the parcel was unintentional and is in that regard indistinguishable from 'inadvertently'. Notice though that in the Menlove case discussed above, we cannot say that Menlove *stacked his hay* inadvertently with the consequence of burning down the cottages. He did *not* stack his hay inadvertently; he *burned down the cottages* inadvertently. So the canceller does not go with the main action. But we can say that the guard pushed the passenger on to the train carelessly. So, the canceller is allowed to go with the main action in the case of carelessness but not in the case of inadvertence. Why should this be the case?

The reason is that in pushing the passenger on to the train carelessly, the guard's negligence was in not attending to *how* he did it. Menlove, on the other hand, probably stacked the hay with great care: he was careful not to swing his fork too wide and careful to produce a stable stack. That is *how* one should stack hay to avoid unwanted results. So if I am criticized for carelessness, the criticism is for the *quality* of the actual execution of the act. If I am criticized for inadvertence, the criticism is for the quality of my attention to the *consequences* of what is otherwise a satisfactory act. This is why the adverb ‘carelessly’ goes with the act that produces the unwanted result (the guard pushed the passenger on to the train carelessly) and why ‘inadvertently’ goes with the unwanted result (Menlove inadvertently burned Vaughan’s cottages); they go with that part of the matter which is the basis of the criticism or excuse. In the case of ‘carelessness’, the adverb goes with the causal act, not its result; in the case of ‘inadvertence’, it goes with the resultant act not its cause.

It seems to be implied in the conceptual independence of these two aberrations that two separate psychological factors are at work: one which, with a regard to consequences, controls the manner of execution of the behaviour (‘you didn’t gauge the distance properly’ or ‘you did it too quickly’ or ‘you didn’t pay attention to what you were doing’); another which controls, with a regard to consequences, the selection of the time and/or place of the behaviour. Both inattention and inadvertence deal with the avoidance and encouragement of certain consequences, perhaps even the same consequences; but each deals, by hypothesis, with a separate way of controlling those consequences. We may say finally that inattention or carelessness refers to the absence of that relation which is required between the cognitive and the physical parts of agency. It is implied that our bodies must be under the control of our cognitive faculties in the fully responsible cases of action.

A schematic representation of carelessness would be as shown in Figure 1.4.

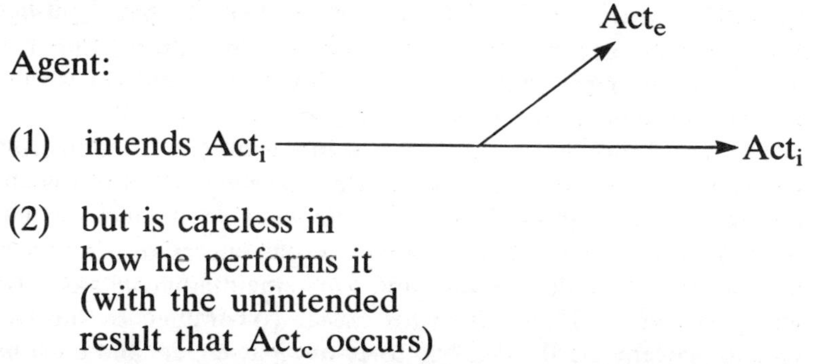

Figure 1.4

The agent intends to do Act_i which he may or may not complete. In the course of it he brings about Act_c due to a lack of care in how he does Act_i.

This completes the class of deviations whose members share the features of being unintentional and are differentiated by the special ways in which the unintentional result is produced.

(5) Involuntariness

We turn then towards the deviation which may be called 'involuntariness'.[7] It differs from the foregoing class in that the involuntary act is intentional. In the hackneyed but paradigmatic case where the agent has a gun held at his head and is thereby forced to commit a wrong such as trespass and theft,[8] he has nevertheless done it intentionally, however unwillingly. Hence the agent's intention is not outwitted by events or let down by ignorance or inattention or lack of attention in performance as it is in accident, mistake, inadvertence and carelessness. What is overridden in cases of involuntariness is his normal selection of goals from among the array normally integral to him.

Consider the following ingredients of our mechanism of choice. There is an ordered set of goals and a means of selecting which of these goals to actuate. The means will include an ability to reckon the consequences of one's choice and to relate the effect of that back to the remainder of one's needs and desires. In the gun-at-the-head sort of case, the preservation of normal choice is overridden in that we are forced to accept the preservation of our own safety at the expense of harming another. We have had our choice constrained by the fact that we cannot preserve our own life unless we harm another. The harm we do to another is then chosen only out of necessity.

There is, however, some difficulty in deciding how extensively this class of aberration is to be allowed to range. What if it is not the will of another, but circumstances which impose the necessity? A ship's officer throws six passengers overboard to avoid the loss of the lifeboat and the remaining crew members and passengers.[9] He has had his choice constrained by the fact that to prevent the death of all forty-one passengers and crew he must throw six overboard. If he chooses the latter, he does so out of necessity. The captain's case and the gun-at-the-head example are both aberrations of choice for the same reasons. In both cases choice is made out of necessity.

Another sort of case is when the agent acts under an internal compulsion, such as kleptomania. Here the agent's desires and needs are, from our point of view, distorted, which results in a malfunction in his capacity to choose. He has as a need what we may have as only a desire. Thus, consequences cannot function for him as they do for us.

Whether, then, it be another's will or motive, or the exigencies of events, or the malfunction of one's own capacity to choose, in each case the agent's choice has been affected in such a way that his own knowledge and preferences and plans or intentions have not been allowed to come to the fore as determinants. The schematic representation of all these cases of involuntariness could then be as shown in Figure 1.5.

Agent:

(1) 'chooses' and

(2) intends $Act_{invol.}$ ⟶ $Act_{invol.}$

but his 'choice' is either

(3) subject to events which require him to 'choose' out of necessity and/or

(4) his ability to reckon the consequences of his 'choice' is itself impaired

Figure 1.5

This means that an agent acts involuntarily when, due to the sort of overriding causes just given, his choice of a goal is produced in such a way that it is not due to that system of actual and potential causes which defines the agent. The agent's normal choice mechanism is thus 'short-circuited' or by-passed, as it were. But his *intention*-forming mechanism goes forward separately and normally. If the agent can be said to have acted involuntarily, he can be said to have intended to achieve the goal he has had imposed upon him; he resolves to act although he has not freely chosen. So involuntary actions are intentional.

Notice that our concept of action has taken another empirical-theoretical position on our psychology: that we have as agents *two* separate mechanisms, one choice-forming and the other resolve-forming. These mechanisms are deemed separable in that when the former is overridden by defect, circumstance, or other agents, the latter need not be. This is another psychological point buried in the phenomenology of our concept of action.

2 THE CONVERSIONS

We can now begin the process of conversion in order to see which features surface as constitutive of non-pathological or standard actions.

The conversions give the following results:

(1a) If I did x *accidentally* then x was the result of an unforeseen event z, which, while I was engaged doing y, so affected events therein that x rather than y resulted.

(1b) If I did x *simpliciter* then (whatever else the doing of x is) it is the result of events foreseen by me. If the act is not, to some reasonable extent, due to events foreseen by me, it becomes an act which is depreciated in some fashion as either lucky or unintentional or perhaps accidental, if the luck is bad. In general, the degree to which the act is due to events not foreseen by me is the degree to which the act becomes less attributable *simpliciter* to me. This suggests that there has to be some workable sense of my having foreseen the events which resulted in x even though, as we know, I cannot have foreseen them all. Some notion like 'relevant, normal (causal) events' will have to be worked out.

(2a) If I did x mistakenly then I had a false belief which was instrumental in the effecting of x. (What is cancelled here is not belief, but true belief.)

(2b) If I did x *simpliciter* then there were instrumental beliefs relevant to the commission of x, and they were true.

(3a) If I did x *inadvertently* then x was the unforeseen result of my having done y.

(3b) If I did x *simpliciter* then if x is a result of something else I have done, y, it is foreseen by me to be a result of y.

(4a) If I did x *carelessly* then it was done without attention to the prevention of undesirable effects which would be due to *how*, with my body, I did x. This is to be distinguished from the standard of care, or, as we prefer, mindfulness, which is that standard which *all* the above abilities of agency, including (4), must meet.

(4b) If I did x *simpliciter* then I did pay proper care and attention to *how* I did x.

(5a) If I did x *involuntarily* then my choices were unavoidably subject to circumstances, agents or a suspension or defect in the mechanism of choice itself.

(5b) If I did x *simpliciter* then my choices resulted from that normally functioning system of causes which we call the Self.

(6a) If I did x *unintentionally* then what occurred was not matched in my intention due to, as we have seen, mistake or inadvertence or carelessness or accident.

(6b) If I did x *simpliciter* then what occurred was, whatever else it was, matched in my intention.

In each of these a-cases (1a-6a) I *did* x, although I did it 'adjustedly'. There is clearly some minimal sense of action still in function in each of these cases and even in some of their combinations.

(7a) Finally, we can say that I did not do x.

7a is the ultimate cancellation, the negation of the concept. It is required in order to bring about whatever (necessary) condition(s) might still be harboured by the ascription of the concept even in its most qualified form.

It must be remembered that the concept of action is still applied in all these cases where an act is done 'adjustedly', that is in all these cases where these positive putative ingredients, 1b-6b, are cancelled. Suppose that A shoots B carelessly and involuntarily while cleaning his gun: what remains of the act? Whatever *not* doing it inadvertently, unintentionally and accidentally would contribute positively. But what if A shot B inadvertently or accidentally and also (therefore) unintentionally? We should still say A shot B. None of the positive conditions so far seems on its own a necessary condition for ascription. Some combination of them might be necessary, but combinations of aberrant actions are difficult to put together because some of the aberrations refer to effects, either of precedent actions or psychological states, and some of them refer to the various other causes of actions. (That is why, if A shoots B carelessly, he could not also do it accidentally.) It seems safe to say that the concept of an action does not require for its adjusted description any of the standard cancellable ingredients as a necessary condition – *ex hypothesi*. The concept of an action ascribed *simpliciter*, however, obviously has all of the standard cancellable ingredients as necessary conditions.

There does seem to be one additional ingredient which is not cancelled by the standard cancellers and which has the status of a necessary condition for the ascription of an action to an agent: my body must stand in a causal relation to any event which is ascribed to me as my action. In the absence of this ingredient the concept of an action cuts out entirely. Thus, a person who is carried on to someone else's land has not performed any action and therefore cannot be liable in trespass.[10]

(7b) If I did x *simpliciter*, then x is an effect of my behaviour.

This, then, is the seventh ingredient of the concept of an action. It is what is represented in our model by the arrow. The list again, of the positive ingredients of an act *simpliciter* is as follows:

(1) Relevant circumstances or causes leading to x are foreseen by me.	('Accident' cancels this feature.)
(2) Relevant true beliefs were in effect.	('Mistake' cancels this.)
(3) I foresaw the relevant effects of my own behaviour.	('Inadvertence' cancels this.)
(4) A certain attention to how it is caused by me was exercised.	('Carelessness' cancels this.)
(5) A normal choice of mine was in effect.	('Involuntariness' cancels this.)
(6) An intention of mine was in effect.	('Unintentional' is the canceller here.)
(7) A certain relevant behaviour of my body was in effect.	(The denial of commission cancels this: 'I didn't do it!')

These are the conditions of the full and favoured case of the concept of an action. We should now say something about the minimal sense of 'action', that sense of action which is still apparently applicable when certain of these seven conditions are absent. The remaining uncancelled conditions will be necessary conditions of a particular action's being ascribed *non-simpliciter*.

We have seen so far that the seventh condition is one necessary condition for an act's being ascribable at all. Is it also sufficient? On the one hand, because we know that x can be done unintentionally, we might want to say that mere behaviour is sufficient for ascription of action. That is, none of the other conditions is required for *simpliciter* ascription since they seem to be severally and jointly cancellable and action still ascribable.

On the other hand, an event which is ascribed to an agent as an act of his and which *appears* unintentional must still be in a clear causal line of descent from an already uncontestably intentional act of the agent. Thus, while x may be done unintentionally, some y must exist which is x's causal ancestor and which is an intentional act of the agent's in order for us to say that the agent did x. Unintentional acts, it seems, are always part of or upshots of actions which are intentional. An accidental act, for example, has as part of its definition that the agent was embarked upon another act which was intended.

At the very least, this view which allows that there are unintentional acts requires that they be dependent upon their relationship with prior intentional acts. There is, however, an attractive position which holds that there exist no unintentional acts whatsoever, that the death of your neighbour's donkey is an *event* not attributable to you as an act but in certain circumstances as a consequence of an act of yours. On this view the concept of an action is not expandable. as it were, creating more and more actions as we uncover more and more events which are relevant to the production of the intended result or are consequences of it.

In an example of Davidson's the question is raised whether in turning on the lights which warned the burglar, the homeowner warned the burglar in the sense that a further and discrete action is ascribable to him. Davidson's view is that such an 'accordion effect'[11] is a misconception.

John's accidentally shooting his neighbour's donkey is, then, not an action additional to what it was that John did that led to the accident, namely, firing his piece with the intention of shooting his own donkey. What 'John's accidentally shooting his neighbour's donkey' is, is a description *put in terms of the consequences of John's singular intentional act of shooting at his own donkey* and a reference to that act by means of its consequential but accidental relation. In this way we refer to one event, in this case an action, by describing another event and its relations to the target event and this second event is not itself an action. An event is thus an act if and only if there is necessarily *some* description under which it is intentional. This 'anti-accordion' view allows us to unify all the descriptions of an action which lack an intentional ingredient, and which some have thought referred to additional actions, under a single ontological particular, namely that single event or set of events which is the action being variously referred to by means of descriptions of related events (which must include the nature of the relation in the description). The alternative, which is to treat each description of an action, even those without the ingredient of intention, as an additional act is to crowd the ontology of action. This crowded view is a result of not having understood the relations between reference and description. The central idea is not to count entities on a one-to-one basis with descriptions since one entity, one event may have countless descriptions.

A reservation about this view of Davidson's is that it requires us to dismiss as an illusion the form of the language in which we apparently phrase some of our descriptions of actions. We do say that John accidentally shot his neighbour's donkey and that form of words is the form we use for intentional acts. Why, we may ask, are certain descriptions phrased in what is apparently action discourse even though they are, according to the hypothesis, (mere) consequences of the seminal act being referred to, while at the same time other descriptions with the same referential function are not in the form of action discourse? One may, for example, refer to the same action with the description 'he accidentally shot his neighbour's donkey' as well as with the description 'the set of events in a certain way causally prior to that donkey's death.' The first description refers to that intentional act which incidentally and accidentally resulted in the wrong donkey's death, but so does the second description. The question is why is the first description set in discourse apparently characteristic of actions?

Given the aims of this treatise we should prefer not to be required by anything we have claimed, or at least had to claim, to take sides on the matter before us of whether there are only intentional acts and all other unintentional and apparent acts are actually descriptions of intentional acts. We believe our views on action to be compatible with both sides. But since we find that our view suggests an answer to the problematic question posed at the end of the last paragraph which is both helpful and consistent with the Davidson position, it is worth our while to pursue this matter for a short time longer.

On our view each action adjuster cancels an essential set of features of an action. Consequently, the description partly concerns the reason why the action has *failed*. These action adjusters are therefore a *specially favoured set of descriptions of actions*. Since these descriptions refer to an action – to what was intended and embarked upon – *by means of those consequences which occurred as a result of the failure of that action*, they are essentially relevant to the question of responsibility and negligence of that action.

But to refer to an action in that special way requires that the action itself figure in the description being used: *it is the way in which the action failed* that is employed as a description. To refer to an action in that special way requires that the consequence of the action, which is the shooting of the neighbour's donkey, be itself referred to in action terms. If we use action discourse to describe the consequence and with the adjuster 'accidentally' both cancel the implication that this was an intentional result and assert that it was because of an unforeseen event that this consequence occurred – all that – then we have described the original action in a most fecund and compact way. We have described the original act from the point of view of an ungoverned or accidental consequence of itself and therewith have raised the questions of responsibility, negligence and culpability. If we were to use sheer event-language to describe the ungoverned consequence and with that to refer, *via* their causal relations, to the original act we should not have as implicative a description of the original act. Suppose that the death of the neighbour's donkey *had* been intended. Then it would be an action and we should want to use action discourse to signify that. To describe that accidental event however as an action, withholding by cancellation only the implication that it was intentional (and/or foreseen), is to leave *in* all the implications we should want to about an event which is a possibly damaging consequence of an act. It leaves in all the questions we should want to raise concerning an event with such relations to an action. This is all compatible, of course, with that accidental event *not* being an action but also with action discourse – properly adjusted, of course – being used in its description. When, then, with *that* description of an action's consequence we refer to that antecedent action-event we are engaged in the use of a favoured description.

That these favoured descriptions are cast in action terms may have, from the Davidson point of view, misled those who took that fact to mean that accidental shootings of donkeys are separately identifiable acts from the doings which, it is argued, preceded them.

The full set of 'favoured descriptions' will be identical with the list of adjusters or types of act-failure we have enumerated.

II

ACTIONS AND DEFENCES

The list of standard deviations or the list of adjusters of action should be complete. If incomplete, the list of main ingredients of the concept of action would be so, as would then be the list of abilities of agents and the definition of agency. One test of completeness resides in the challenge to produce relevant deviations not yet represented in the list of adjusters. Some positive evidence that the list is complete would be that all legal defences are relatable to the features of agency. If we could show that all existing legal defences are explainable and/or predictable on the basis of the absence of various features of agency, we should have a theoretical link between agency and the legal defences. This test of completeness assumes that the list of legal defences is complete. Since none of them is really recent – they are all actually relatively venerable – the assumption seems workable at this stage. There again, however, the final test must be in terms of a challenge: produce further legal defences which are not relatable as these are, to the features of action or agency.[1]

Related, as we have seen, to the concern over completeness of the features of action is an interest in the theoretical or explanatory relations between the concept of agency and legal defences. We expect that the features of agency will explain why defences are defences and will thus inform the law at a level on which it has not yet been self-conscious.

We intend now to apply certain aspects of the concept of action to the defences in tort and criminal law. The acts with which we will be dealing will all be unlawful, for only then will defences be relevant.

The theory, in accordance with common legal belief, holds that for the class of standardly performed unlawful acts, no defence exists. If, however, the act can be shown to be non-standard in some respect, if, that is, the presence of at least one adjuster can be established, then legal culpability may be diminished. The theory explains this by showing how agency is diminished when we do something accidentally, mistakenly, carelessly, inadvertently or involuntarily. Diminished agency and therefore the possibility of diminished legal culpability occurs in each of the first four classes of cases because of the absence of intention. As Holmes is reported to have told us, 'Even a dog [distinguishes in agency] between being kicked and being stumbled over.'[2] Diminished agency occurs in the fifth class of cases, that of involuntaries, because of the absence of the free reign of choice.

What we seek to be protected from is both intentional and unintentional damaging events. We protect ourselves from intentionally produced damaging events by declaring them criminally and civilly unlawful. The absence of voluntariness or of intent is generally a defence against such crimes or torts. We protect ourselves against unintentional damaging events by demanding, through the law of civil and criminal negligence, a standard of mindfulness in agents. By doing so, we can hope to minimize the flow of damage from our actions.

Table 2.1 lists the elements of a standard action and the basic defences of the criminal and civil law, and correlates them by showing which element of a standard action is negated by which defences.

Given (7), certain relevant behaviour of body in effect, defences fall into three categories. The first are defences which negate one or more of (1) to (6) because of insanity or infancy, etc., by showing lack of capacity. Lack of capacity functions as a defence because rules cannot affect the conduct of persons who do not have at least a minimum capacity of agency. The classic formulation of the defence of insanity is that of Lord Chief Justice Tindal in *Daniel M'Naghten's* case[3] where he stated that

> the jurors ought to be told in all cases that every man is to be presumed to be sane, and to possess a sufficient degree of

Table 2.1

Defences which function by negating one or more of (1) to (6)	*The elements of a standard action*	*Defences of no intent or* mens rea *by negating of any of (1) to (4), directly*
	(1) Relevant circumstances or causes foreseen	– accident (inevitable) or otherwise)
	(2) Relevant true beliefs in effect	– mistake of fact
– insanity – infancy – intoxication – automatism – provocation	(3) Relevant effects foreseen	– no foresight
	(4) Standard of attention was in effect	– inattention, or body not under the control of the relevant other elements of action
	(5) If 1 to 4 then an intention was in effect	– denial of (5) by a negation of (1)-(4)
	(6) Normal choice in effect	*Defences which negate (6)* – necessity – self-defence – defence of third persons – defence of property – compulsion – coercion
Defence of alibi or 'I didn't do it' by denial of (7)	(7) Certain relevant behaviour of body in effect	

reason to be responsible for his crimes, until the contrary be proved to their satisfaction; and that to establish a defence on the grounds of insanity, it must be clearly proved that, at the time of the committing of the act, the party accused was labouring under such a defect of reason, from disease of the mind, as not to know the nature and quality of the act he was doing; or, if he did know it, that he did not know he was doing what was wrong.

The defence of insanity is a good vehicle to demonstrate the practicability of our analysis of action.

The key terms in the M'Naghten formulation and definitions of insanity derived from it are hopelessly vague. We can have only the dimmest idea of what 'disease of the mind' and 'wrong' mean. Experts from relevant areas can be consulted, but that will probably not help. There is no reason to believe that a psychiatrist's technical sense of these crucial terms would have the right bearing on the cognate legal concepts and the policies which inform their meaning. If, however, we employ the criteria offered by our theory of action, we can instruct the non-legal expert in a way which allows him to make his evidence germane to the legal questions. Thus, we begin with a theory of what is legally relevant in action and ask our questions of the expert fact-suppliers from that standpoint rather than accepting by default a professional definition which may very well be motivated by quite different considerations (if any) from those of the law.

We know that the elements of the offence comprise the constituents of the definitions of standard actions:

(i) relevant circumstances or causes are foreseen,
(ii) relevant effects of the actor's behaviour are foreseen,
(iii) a particular standard of care and attention is exercised,
(iv) relevant true beliefs are employed,
(v) a normal choice was in effect.

Insanity may negate a standard action by bringing any or all of the adjusters into play; it may negate the capacity to foresee consequences of conduct or the capacity to exercise due care, or produce a mistaken belief in the state of things, or impair the agent's capacity to choose between goals. The defence illustrates the policy of the law of not rendering agents criminally responsible for non-standard actions.

The defence of automatism, which is merely action without conscious volition, rests on its negating or sufficiently diminishing all the elements of standard action except bodily movement. Thus, the standard action theory readily meets the needs of these defences (insanity, intoxication and automatism) and provides more readily applicable indices for their operation.

In regard to the intentional torts and the criminal law, there is a further set of defences which can all be explained by means of the adjuster 'involuntarily'. These are the defences of necessity, self-defence, defence of others, defence of property, and compulsion and coercion. In all these defences, circumstances have placed the actor in a situation where he must choose from among negative alternatives. His normal choice mechanism has been overridden. Although he has chosen to obtain the minimum negative balance, his choice is non-standard. Defences which negate (6), normal choice in effect, by establishing some sort of justification such as necessity, presuppose the ability of agents to calculate and choose.

The third category of defence negates intent by establishing the presence of accident, mistake, carelessness, or inadvertence. For an event to be called the action of an agent it must be an effect which can be traced to certain of his powers of agency. Given that intention we expect agents to employ some standards in the exercise of their powers of agency in order to assure that damaging consequences will be avoided. While intent may be negated, a lesser degree of culpability will remain if a minimum standard is not exercised by the agent in his actions. When matters have occurred which were beyond the scope of the agent's abilities to have foretold, we accept that such effects were not eliminable. Therefore we count them as beyond the effective standard of mindfulness by means of the resources available to us in controlling agency.

The theory of actions allows us to distinguish three concepts: responsibility, culpability or fault, and agency. The ascription of some responsibility to an agent requires a causal connection between the act (or event) in question and the agent's body and some features of his agency. Agency, according to the analysis, is that set of causes which would produce the required features of a standard action. An agent is in some degree responsibile so long as the event in question may be causally traced to him and certain features of his agency, no matter how long the causal tracing. But responsibility by itself would not imply culpability (or blame or fault). Responsibility would imply a causal relationship while culpability would imply a form of control according to that policy, which is central to the concept of action, for example, that of anti-negligence. Agents are required to meet a standard of mindfulness in order to minimize the occurrence of undesirable consequences which otherwise might flow as effects from their projects or plans. So to know that an agent is responsible is to know only that he stands as a causal antecedent in his capacity as an agent to an event and that he is therefore reachable by our policy. To know that an agent is culpable or at fault is to know that he is responsible *and* that he has acted below the standard of mindfulness we require; it is to find him to have thwarted the goals of our policy and therefore to be subject to its remedies. We, in effect, now reach back to the criticizable aspects of his agency in the event in question.

The question of how far culpability is to run down the causal chain of responsibility – how far responsibility determines culpability – is known as the remoteness problem in law. We do know that if an agent, A, plans an act, *a*, and *b* results accidentally, we will hold A culpable for *b* if it should have been foreseen by him. His negligence is what we want to eliminate by such policy. But what if *c* now occurs as the result of *b* and is totally unforeseeable? The theory tells us that A is responsible for *c*; he does stand in the right causal ancestry of agency back through *b* to his plan for *a*. But is he culpable? This is the question to which we now address ourselves.

For any negligent act there are generally certain harmful effects which are foreseeable in the particular. These effects constitute the risk, and determine the standard of care to be applied. When these effects materialize as a result of an action, remoteness is not a defence. These effects cannot be too remote because they are the very things which the actor ought to have had in mind in acting.

There are other effects, however, which could not be said to be reasonably foreseeable. It is in regard to these that the defence of remoteness of damage might be raised. While these effects may not be reasonably foreseeable in and of themselves, they may, nevertheless, belong to a *class* of effects which is foreseeable. You can have foreseeability in terms of a singular description of events, and you can have foreseeability in terms of a general description of events.

The following are the major categories of general classes of events where foreseeability of the particular damage is not necessary for recovery in the law of negligence:

Dangerous activities

It is a fact of life that damage can materialize from dangerous or damaging events in a variety of ways, and that these damaging events can lead to other damaging events. The fact that we judge an action to be negligent in terms of the risks which have the highest probabilities should not be allowed to free negligent actors from liability for damage of a lower probability in the particular, if the class of which it is a member has a fair degree of probability in terms of foreseeability.

If a person drives while intoxicated at 90 miles an hour down the wrong side of the street and sideswipes an oncoming car, he will be found culpable and liable to pay for the damage. If he strikes an oncoming car in a head on collision and kills six passengers, we would find him equally culpable, and liable for the full amount of the damage. There is no difference in degrees of culpability in a case where the driver merely sideswiped an oncoming car, or destroyed it, killing a carload of passengers. The amount of damage done is a matter of good or bad luck. Equally if the intoxicated driver careened off the road, hit a fence and popped out the staples, which were then eaten by cattle resulting in their loss due to contracting hardware disease, that concatenation would also be a matter of chance.[4] Whether or not a negligent dangerous act results in other 'possible' damaging events which are not reasonably foreseeable in the particular, is purely a matter of chance. The culpability is the same because of the likelihood of a wide unspecified variety of similar events the set of which is foreseeable.

The thin skull case

It is clearly foreseeable that people have different susceptibilities to damaging events, both physically and mentally. These may be the result of genetic abnormalities, illness, physical handicaps, or disease. Although no particular susceptibility will be foreseeable, the reasonable possibility of some kind of susceptibility clearly is. Consequently the law provides that the negligent actor must 'take his victim as he finds him'. Damage due to the existence of a particular physical or mental susceptibility is thus not too remote.

Medical complications

The potential for unforeseen medical complications as the result of an injury is clearly reasonably foreseeable. The complications may arise in the natural course of the illness. They might be the result of the treatment for the injury, whether or not the treatment itself was properly or negligently carried out. Complications may also arise as a result of further injury brought about by the initial damaging event. A person who has had his leg broken may break his other leg because of the handicap of the first break. While no single such event may have been foreseeable, the possibility of complications of this nature are entailed by any risk of serious physical harm.

Rescue

Whenever any person is put into a dangerous situation as a result of a negligent act, it is reasonably foreseeable that people will come to his aid, if given the opportunity, and in doing so will put themselves under a risk of harm. It is not foreseeable that on a particular occasion a particular person may stop to render aid to people injured in a motor vehicle accident, but it is reasonably foreseeable that persons do come to the aid of others under such circumstances, and in doing so will be in danger of injury. Injury invites rescue, and some rescue invites injury.

Nervous shock

The suffering of nervous shock as the result of witnessing an injury to another or arriving upon the aftermath of an injury, is the kind of thing which is reasonably foreseeable in general, but not necessarily so in any particular case. It is not so frequent as can be said to be reasonably foreseeable in each particular case, but happens often enough so that it is a distinct foreseeable possibility in general. Such damage is not held by the law to be too remote providing that nervous shock is suffered by a close relative such as spouse or parent, and the shock is suffered as a result of witnessing the accident, or seeing the victims of the accident in a bloodied or injured state.

An analysis by the authors of the negligence cases raising remoteness issues, decided by the courts of England, Canada, Australia and New Zealand, from the latter part of the nineteenth century up to the present, shows that in regard to damage suffered by plaintiffs which falls within each of the above classes, in 90 per cent of the cases the damages were found to not be too remote irrespective of whether the judges purported to use a causation or foreseeability test.[5] From this study we can conclude that damages which are foreseeable in the particular, or as a member of a foreseeable class of damages, are not too remote, while damages which are not foreseeable in the particular, or do not fall within a foreseeable class, are too remote. Foreseeability limits the range of culpability down the causal chain, because it marks the outer limit of the agent's ability to prevent the harmful consequences of his actions.

Turning to the more general defence of absence of *mens rea*, in the criminal law, we find that the standard action theory is of considerable assistance in removing the conceptual vagueness that clouds the criminal law. *Mens rea* can refer to a particular state of mind that the prosecution must prove before its case is established, or it can mean moral culpability, the absence of which will excuse the accused.[6] The legal descriptions of *mens rea* are essentially subjective and uncertain and usually fail to set out the criteria of culpability. But on the standard action theory *mens rea* is implicit in a standard action, and its presence or absence depends upon presence or absence of certain adjusters. Putting it another way, the prosecutor can always establish a *mens rea* by establishing the absence of certain adjusters, if policy dictates the burden of proof should be on the prosecution. This enables us to dispense with problematic distinctions such as those between intention and recklessness[7] while maintaining workable distinctions such as those of advertence as opposed to inadvertence.

How does our theory relate to the significant burden of proof elements in the criminal process? Criminal law generally places the burden of proof of all the elements of a crime on the prosecution, subject to narrow and specific exceptions. Under the standard action theory, if the facts raise a *prima facie* case of presence of a standard action, the burden of introducing evidence to prove the contrary would generally fall on the accused. And if the facts raise a *prima facie* inference of the existence of an adjuster then the burden of disestablishing its presence would rest on the prosecution.

More specifically, the burden of proof in relation to the three recognized classes of criminal offences can be stated in the following way:

(a) *Offences requiring proof of* mens rea[8]
The onus is on the prosecution to establish the absence of adjusters, except in cases of involuntariness.
(b) *Offences requiring proof of criminal negligence*
One or more of the adjusters of (1) to (4) are assumed, but the onus is on the prosecution to establish culpability.
(c) *Strict liability offences*[9]
The prosecution must prove the act, or the seventh ingredient of an action, namely, relevant bodily movement, and the accused must prove one or more adjusters and no culpability.
(d) *Absolute liability offences*
The prosecution must prove the act, the seventh ingredient of action. The accused must prove adjuster (5), involuntariness.

The arguments which provide one with an excuse in the law are similar to those which provide one with an excuse in our theory. The presence of an adjuster is exculpatory in the law in the same way as in the theory. The features of action are identical for both the theory and the law, and the law assumes the same psychology as does the theory. For these reasons the standard action theory helps us to clarify and resolve many difficult legal theoretical disputes, only some of which have been addressed in this chapter. Its essential simplifying quality rests on its capacity to organize around a theory what are otherwise vague and loosely related legal concepts.

Having argued from the legal side that the list of action adjusters is complete, since they properly match and explain the legal defences, we may now return to the main road of our argument.

III

AGENTS AND RIGHTS

The standard position on what constitutes a fundamental right is that it is identical with a justified or valid basic claim.[1] The trouble with this view is that, unless it tells us what proper justification is, we are no further along. Another, possibly related view, that our basic rights reside in the preservation of the respect and concern[2] for the individual, is equally uninformative until we are given an account of them, and it must be remembered that the accounts of the justification of claims of respect or of concern have to be sufficiently inter-subjective to allow the existence of such public institutions as the law and morality.

There cannot be much doubt that any account of rights will, as the above incomplete views themselves attest, have to come from some position about what is vital to agents. Our position on what actions imply about agents may find us well placed to make somewhat more explicit the venerable connection between the basic nature of agents and their basic rights.[3] We may begin with the question of what abilities our agents must have in order to perform an act standardly. It is after all agents who are the final subjects of laws and it is their abilities which are the subject of cancellation or diminution by adjusters and therefore upon which defences rest.

If then, an agent must be able to foresee the relevant circumstances or causes leading to an objective and foresee the relevant effects of his own behaviour then he must (a) be able to reckon and predict and perform other such mental operations. If relevant true beliefs must be in effect as they perform actions, agents must (b) be able to appraise the truth of propositions. If a certain standard of care and attention must be exercisable then agents must (a) be able to predict consequences of their behaviour, (b) to appraise the truth of propositions, and (c) be capable of having objectives, needs and desires. If he is capable of voluntary actions he will (d) be able to choose and order his objectives. And if certain relevant bodily behaviour of his must be in effect in a standard action and under the control of the other aspects of agency, under the control, that is, of his cognitive faculties, then he must (e) be capable of actuating his objectives or initiating events which will bring them about. This set of five features defines the abilities of agents or what is essential to their agency. They seem to be essential to the concept of agency while other features of agency seem to be derivable from them. It is also these features and apparently only these which make us subject to praise and blame. And it is these features which, if we reflect, define our true individuality. This list of abilities may be re-ordered and amplified as follows.

(1) the ability to evaluate the truth of empirical propositions;
(2) the ability to reckon, which includes prediction, numerateness and logic and is not separable from the first ability;
(3) the capacity of having goals, where this will mean that our needs and desires function in some way as background to our goals;
(4) the (at least partial) ability to choose among these *desiderata* by ranking them according to their consequences and relative desirability, thus using (1) and (2), and thereby forming plans and having resolves;
(5) the ability to set in motion, with one's body, events which tend to accomplish these objectives.

An agent then is a sentient, reckoning, goal-oriented, physically effective system.

Clearly, the third ingredient contains the heart of such a system. The other features are each expressible as means to it or some member of it. But those features of agency (1), (2), (4) and (5) are for our purposes central for just that reason. All agents will want these features of theirs to be allowed to function maximally in the satisfaction of the givens of the third feature, whatever they may be. Our most basic *common* interest then is to see that the individual 'enabling' features of agency are maximized. We can see that this will be independent of named *desiderata*, other than that of the effectiveness of agency. It is reasonable then that this set of features will comprise our basic political and/or legal rights: they are fundamental for each agent if he is to be able to do what he wants, *whatever* that is. Clearly, the third ingredient cannot be ignored. The way in which it works will emerge shortly.

1

We have then one major criterion which is selective of basic rights: whatever is *enabling* of the agent's ability to pursue his particular interests, independently of whatever they actually turn out to be. This is the right to action not including its actual goal – it is the right to *actability*. It is the right to agency purified of particular teleology.

This hypothesis allows us to predict that the most well-known and agreed-upon basic rights will match up with our basic abilities as actors. The first two abilities of agents are concerned with the truth of propositions and we may therefore call them the epistemological conditions of action. We may predict that certain epistemological rights will exist in order to protect those conditions of action. Rights to freedom of the press, to assembly, to freedom of thought and speech are clearly epistemological in character and relate in a basic way to the possibility of action. The right to freedom of movement is the right that the fifth ability of agency, that of physical effectiveness, is unhampered. The right to individual happiness is the right that our individual teleology or choice of projects be exercisable.

We have then epistemological, teleological and physical rights as agents *because the abilities protected by those rights define us as agents*. We have thus the right to be agents, to be what we are. We have the right to act.

The correlative duty, which the right to act implies, is the familiar negative duty, that we not impede the acts of others, *ceteris paribus*. This consideration gives us the other major criterion of basic rights: what they require reciprocally as duties is 'negative' action. Our basic rights protect our ability to do things and this means protecting those abilities which enable us to act standardly, and thus, as we have seen, freely. The basic right of liberty or freedom amounts to this: the right, (*ceteris paribus*), to express our teleologies, to act unimpeded by the actions, of other agents.

The negative duties of non-interference which are implied by and are necessary conditions for the rights which constitute our basic freedoms of action are the subject matter of the law of delict or tort. A breach of these duties will give rise to a cause of action which will generally fall within the ambit of one or more torts such as assault, battery, false imprisonment, negligent interference with or harm to the person, malicious prosecution, intimidation, invasion of privacy, or the intentional infliction of mental suffering.

We see that the very idea of a right implies protection. Moreover, the implication is of a *right* to protection or enforcement.[4] The natural right to the expression of our agency implies then the natural meta-right to the enforcement of those rights. In the state of nature we may each rightfully engage in our own forms of protection. As we move toward rule-governedness we may delegate the work and right of enforcement, perhaps retaining, as even Hobbes did, the rights to some ultimate types of enforcement, such as self-defence, for ourselves.

2

Agents have then the right-to-do X or not-to-do X and the duty-not-to-do-what would prevent another from the exercise of that disjunctive right. That right and duty are contrastable with the right that X be done by another and, its semantic equivalent, the duty of another that X be done. Once our basic rights as agents are set in place a sequence develops which in the service of the extension of agency introduces a supplementary area of rights. Our individual abilities to appraise the truth values of propositions, to reason and predict, to choose and be the cause of our choices' eventuation are extended by the creation of agencyenhancing practices. These practices are those of truth-telling, reasonableness, contract and proprietariness. Each of these activities, we shall argue, is justified with respect to the basic features of agency. It is their direct contribution to what each of us essentially is which connects the notion of obligation to these practices.

3

(1) Truth-telling

In order to extend the ability to appraise the truth-value of propositions upon which, as we have seen, the ability to choose and therefore to act in accordance with our intention rests, reliance upon the abilities of others is needed. If the assertions of each of us may be counted upon to be truthful it is clear that the agency of each of us will have been enormously extended. The practice that we speak, not tell, the truth, is our means to this. The obligation to speak the truth has its legal counterpart in the law of delict or torts, particularly the areas of fraud or deceit, injurious falsehood, passing off, and other unlawful trade practices such as false advertising, the law of defamation, and negligent misrepresentation.

(2) Rationality

The practice of truth-speaking implies that agents must be able to reckon, must be rational, since the appraisal of the truth-value of beliefs will depend upon our ability to reckon according to certain rules. The first practice will then call forth a second, that of what we may call formal rationality. If, for example, prediction is a requirement of rationality in that we must have class terms in order to reason, it will also be the case that these terms must be used consistently. Prediction and truth will both depend upon such considerations, among others, from formal rationality. We may not require that the actions of agents always meet this set of rationality conditions; they may be as formally irrational as they choose except when their actions affect others. In the latter case we find them obliged to act within those norms of formal rationality since otherwise neither we nor they may predict the consequences upon us, consequences being known (best) through prediction. Since prediction presupposes predication, universalizability (consistency), impartiality and other canons of formal rationality, we can see that formal rationality is a necessary condition of the function of any social practice or institution. We shall return to this in special connection with law when we look at the principles of formal justice.

(3) Contract

We do through the requirement of truth-speaking extend our agency through increased knowledge derived from other agents who are party to the practice. We are in this way able to learn of their future actions, which is often of signal importance, as they truly relate their intentions. But if we were able to *effect*, not merely learn of, the future voluntary actions of other agents, the increase in our ability to effect our own choices would be dramatically extended. Promising and its legal counterpart, contract, is the artifact constructed for this purpose. It is a way to gain a co-ordination of goals between agents in order to increase the means, through a commitment to certain actions, by which we may mutually achieve our ends; thus both the extension of relations between agents and the increased availability of ends to agents. We shall extend the idea of contract in the latter portions of this chapter.

Voluntary undertakings upon which reliance can reasonably be placed create enforceable obligations at law, whether they are simple promises or complex commercial transactions. The law of contracts in the civil law tradition is broader than at common law in that the civil law will enforce unilateral promises (undertakings without reciprocal consideration) while at common law breach of such undertakings give rise to liability in tort for losses through reliance. Through contract people can secure the benefits of almost any kind of lawful behaviour from others. Bodies of law have developed around kinds of behaviour which agents find particularly valuable or desirable in pursuit of their own objectives. Contractual forms evolve along with sets of rules which can stabilize expectations to a high degree. These make up such areas of the law as commercial transactions, secured transactions, insurance, or marriage contracts.

(4) Proprietariness

There is no doubt that our actions are proprietary. They are *individuated* with respect to the agents who perform them and they are describable as the action of that agent. Their individuation determines their proprietariness. If we have any idea at all of proprietariness it begins there. But an action may have consequences which go beyond the action, particularly if our theory of action has acts, as acts, cease with the bodily movements of the agent (or even earlier), all further else being ascribed to consequence. It does not seem that a notion of proprietariness may easily be made to cross the gap from action to consequence merely because of the proprietariness of the action. Because the act is yours then the consequence is, is a venerable argument with an intuitive ring but not yet conclusive. It takes, from our point of view, an argument which goes back to the aetiological vitals of agency, to the particulars constitutive of action. We suggest the following. Agents have needs and goals and know they have needs and goals which take recurring satisfaction. Food, shelter and such are obvious but only common examples. Since the motivation may, with memory, be more or less permanent and the satisfaction is achievable through objects which may permanently satisfy the permanent needs then the goal of the effort will be to achieve some permanent connection with these objects. That is the source of proprietariness.

In the absence of somehow making room for an intentional, permanent connection with these objects of our interest we would force agents to act again and again, each day anew as it were, always only in the temporary satisfaction of their permanent needs. They would not be able to match permanence of need with some degree of permanence of satisfaction. A way of accommodating this concept of permanence of relationship with a source of satisfaction is what the practice of proprietariness is meant to serve. This concept holds no implication for the exclusivity or inclusivity of the relation or for the nature of the *relata*. Which conditions we choose to add to the essential relation will be subject to factors which are determined by the further interest of agents in relation to what is possible with others. But some notion of proprietariness which has the minimum content we describe is called for as an extension of the basic teleological feature of agency. It is an extension of agency since it allows us not merely to pursue our goals, to be teleological systems, but to achieve a connection with at least certain of our goals which is *respected* as permanent. That permanence of relation is itself a basic *desideratum*; but since proprietariness is a function of the attitudes and actions of others it cannot be achieved outside of a practice wherein expectations and sanctions work together. The distinction then between merely having permanent possession of an object and proprietariness is that with the latter there is a duty of non-interference with the possession. This will be in the interest of every agent since it creates an item which may now appear in the choice-system of every agent and it is an item which is of ubiquitously high priority which would otherwise not exist for all agents.

A wide variety of proprietary practices have evolved within a legal framework, which agents can voluntarily invoke or participate in to extend their agency. These include such rule-governed activities as conveying, bequeathing, leasing, lending and mortgaging. Through these and other similar practices many different property interests can be created. Estates in land such as fee simples, life estates, leasehold estates and reversions, and other interests such as trusts, tenancies in common or joint tenancies, easements and profits à prendre are only a few. Our property relationships are protected through a variety of torts which provide the necessary conditions for a cause of action to arise for interference with those relations. These include the law of trespass, nuisance, *Rylands* v. *Fletcher* (a special form of strict liability), conversion, detinue, bailment, passing-off and the law of restitutions and unjust enrichment.

4

We may now begin to summarize our findings concerning both

basic rights and their extensions. From the basic features of agents which were abilities or capacities with respect to:

(1) truth
(2) reason
(3) goals
(4) choice
(5) causal efficacy

we derived the rights to freedom of thought, speech, the press, and association, from concern for (1); rights to be free of assault, coercion or injury from concern for (3), (4) and (5); the right to be free of unjustifiable imprisonment from (3), (4) and (5); and the right to happiness or the right to freedom of action, which would imply freedom of choice, from (1), (2), (3), (4) and (5).

The extensions of these abilities, accomplished through the institution of voluntary practices, gave us the additional rights through these practices that:

(1) speakers speak the truth;
(2) agents employ the canons of reason when the interests of others are foreseeably involved;
(3) agents complete upon their contracts or promises;
(4) agents respect the objects of our proprietary interests.

This last list of rights is a set which is semantically equivalent to others having these duties-to-do for us. Of course they only have these duties when they voluntarily come under the respective practices. This list of rights-that-others-do, exists, we know, only in that a set of rights-to-do or not-to-do exists. That presupposed set is the right to voluntarily invoke the practices within which the above rights-that-others-do are set, namely, the practices of truth-speaking, rationality, contract and proprietariness. The choice to perform such actions as come under these practices obviously did not exist prior to the creation of the practices.

It will be noticed that the abilities of agents appear to be expressed as abilities to perform under the above practices. This may seem to be a difficulty in that the practices are argued for as if they are created subvenient to the abilities of agents and in support of them. What our argument needs in order to survive is the notion of some core of abilities which agents have and which is essential to the constitutions of the practices. Once that is accepted we may express even the idea of agency in terms of the practices since that will include the separate core of agency abilities.

5

Agents will voluntarily embark upon courses of actions which are subject to the practices only if they know that the requirements which are made of them are subject to certain constraints. Agents must know that the administration of the voluntary practices will be, at the least, rational since that is a condition of predictability. It will be useful then to examine the so-called 'Formal Principles of Justice' which are the administrative rules of the practice of law and therefore probably of all practices. These principles are as follows:

(1) *The doctrine of precedent*
Relevantly like cases shall be decided alike.

(2) *The duty to be impartial*
No judge who himself is a party to, or has a direct pecuniary interest in, or who has motives for prejudice or bias in regard to any proceedings shall be qualified to adjudicate in those proceedings.

(3) *The rule of law*
Those who create and administer the law are subject to the law.

(4) *The right to due process of law*
No person may be lawfully deprived of any right except through legal processes which are the same for everyone in similar relevant circumstances.

(5) *Equality before the law*
All members of the set coming before the law will be treated equally by the law; and irrelevant properties of members will be identifiable once the set is identified.

(6) *The reciprocity of rights and duties*
Rights and duties are reciprocal in that any agent who has duties imposed upon him by the law shall enjoy the rights furnished by the law, and any agent who enjoys rights

under the law shall be bound by the duties imposed by the law.

We can see that (1) follows from the principle of reason that unless we employ predicates and other terms in a consistent manner we have neither consistency in, nor predictability from, our arguments. Since these are epistemological conditions of an action, a practice which lacked them could not claim to be voluntary. The second principle is implied by the first since partiality is the enemy of consistency. If the legal officials are not subject to law they are not subject to rationality nor to the other rights and duties stemming from the defence and voluntary extension of agency: hence three. The fourth and sixth principles are also applications of consistency, while the fifth argues that where some content is necessary in order to define 'citizen', and consistency is a requirement, irrelevancies will be identifiable.

Once the content is supplied upon which these principles of consistency are to work, their statement becomes practical. We, of course, have argued that the basic legal predicate, the basic class term of constitutions, is, or ought to be, a term with the content we have ascribed to agency. The central strategy of our argument has been that all basic relevant considerations which appear in law (perhaps in morals as well) are either direct expansions of agency or justifiable by it. This tactic is at work even on the principles of formal justice.

6

It may have already been noticed that we appear to have used two models of practices, one which has force only upon a voluntary move to enter the activities, to take on the duties and rights, of the practice, and another which seems to have no such condition of voluntary invocation. The practice of truth-speaking and the others are of the first sort while the rights and negative duties which protect agency itself seem to lack the requirement of voluntary entrance. Nevertheless we cannot say that we come upon those rights and duties of the second sort, those claims for and upon our actions, involuntarily. These rights and duties define the freedom of agents and therefore imply voluntariness.

Voluntary acquiescence to the principles of voluntariness is unnecessary.

Tellingly, however, legislative activities exist which impose, through sanctions, requirements upon agents which do not appear to gain their authority from the voluntary acceptance by agents. No clear public and datable events which signal the voluntary commitment to come under the regulations and sanction of such 'authority' are produceable. But if the activities of legislatures can be seen as comprising a practice which falls into that set which is justified as an extension to agency then their authority would be clear. It would stem from the free exercise of agency as have all the values and procedures gathered in this chapter so far.

Before we look at legislation from the point of view of agency one more implication should be emphasized. Agency implies the right-to-do (or not-to-do). This implies a set of interests or values which is indexed by the choices to-do which agents freely make. The existence of this set, whose ramifications are the topic of the immediately succeeding chapters, contains the ground upon which conflicts among agents will occur. Up to this point, we have described interests which are common to all agents. All agents will want the grounds of action protected and extended; but agents will very likely differ in the *exercise* of their teleologies. They will have different needs, and that, with some scarcity assumed, will provide one basis of conflict. Another basis of conflict will be due to the opposite fact that we have many identical ends, which increases the likelihood of relevant scarcity and therefore conflict.

Early in the history of the development of the concept of agency our conceptual ancestors would have seen that conflict confined the area within which agency could function. If agency was to extend itself beyond the obvious physical limits which conflict imposes, such practices as negotiation and contract would be needed. We are able to extend our agency into the area of conflict by negotiating/contracting (n/c) with as many other agents as may affect our interests adversely. Our previous discussion of contract dealt with the extension of agency into the area of co-operation where our interests are served by the n/c possibility with as many other agents as may affect our interests positively.

The actual shape of the n/c practice will be determined by the number of agents and other complicating factors. In principle each and all agents could n/c for themselves. In practice, especially given certain identities of interests, agents may tend to delegate n/c activities. An example of the above is furnished by the legal practice of appointing agents to act for one in negotiating contracts. The very fact that the term 'agent' is used in this particular context as 'one who acts for another' is revealing. There are times when our own goals and objectives are better achieved for us by allowing others to not only negotiate for us but to allow them to reach and make agreements which bind us without our approval of the terms which they have negotiated. Thus 'agency' in its legal usage is merely an extension of the practice of contracting.

Where the sheer number of agents who have an interest in co-operative effort in achieving shared goals, and in negotiating conflicts over scarce resources, prevents each agent negotiating for himself, groups of agents sharing common interests, can, as principals, appoint an agent to negotiate for them as a group. Numbers may dictate that an adequate representation of the interests of all participating agents may be such that their representatives may even be too numerous to reach a unanimous consensus among themselves. By prior agreement on a decision procedure, such as an agreement to be bound by the majority vote, even large n/c bargaining processes are possible. This allows a further extension of our individual agency. Legislating, when viewed as a complex practice incorporating a set of sub-practices such as n/c, 'agents' acting for principles, and decision by majority vote, can thus be viewed as extending agency, and is thus consistent with autonomy, and consequently legitimate. Contractarians may see legislatures in this light: as contractual-negotiating pits.

Most, perhaps all, contractarians, from Hobbes to Rawls, believe that our minimal political contracts must contain certain preconceived terms. Hobbes believed that agents must surrender all autonomy, Rawls that they must commit themselves to certain distributional rights and duties. Our view is that only the n/c practice itself, initially devoid of any content, is implied as an extension of agency. What the practice of n/c may then produce is another matter. No *social* contract, where that implies some content which functions as a precondition on what may emerge, is implied. Our argument takes us to the *nature* of the practices implied, not to the content which may be negotiated by their use.

Agency on this view remains supreme although the necessities produced by the competitive agency of others become a salient factor in the reckonings of all agents. This expresses itself in the creation of the n/c practice. Without this essential political practice, the claim is that we should find our agency with less impact, less ability to be exercised, than with it.

A consequence of this is that legislatures are not sovereign. They are a *particular* form which the n/c practice has taken and are therefore no more supreme than that practice whose subordination to agency is clear from which factor is the end and which the means to the other, a matter we examine at length in the ensuing chapter. Where arguments from agency may be made, legislatures are consequently not free to act against them. This suggests again that our enterprise in this treatise is not entirely descriptive. But since there appears anyway to be an area of confusion surrounding the role of legislatures, it being described as sovereign, while each person is also held to be free, some prescription may not be unwanted.

We turn now to face further intricacies of the main practices, or rule-governed activities, or extensions of agency, which constitute the law. One of our main concerns as we examine the rule-governed activities of adjudication and legislation will be the problems internal to any such activity, *including* the activity of being an agent. This is the problem of the relationship between rules, which constitute the central form of agency-extension, and their purposes.

IV

THE POSITIVIST'S FEAR

1

We have argued in Chapter III that the practices of truth-speaking, contract and property were natural developments of agency. They are literal extensions of it, increasing the Epistemological, Teleological and Physical (ETP) abilities. Each of these practices, however, is rule-governed. The practice of truth-speaking, for example, will presuppose a language, itself a rule-governed activity, among which will be rules for the application of truth-values to its propositions. Without regulative rules by means of which the actions of others are made highly predictable, these practices could not furnish a useful basis for the extension of agency. In each case the rules provide the basis for the set of true beliefs which agents will use to inform their actions. We know from Chapter I how true beliefs form a necessary part of (standard) action. Rule-governedness, thought of for the moment as devoid of external purpose, has itself the one main purpose which is to add that extra E-dimension which is necessary for the serious extension of agency. Laws and rules in general may be seen as the form which any extension of agency will take so long as human behaviour remains so startlingly regulatable. Rule-governedness is the essence of any practice, game or other artifacted activity just because it provides the necessary epistemic base from which those actions and others newly created by the practice are possible.

Provided that other things are at least equal, this extension of the range of true beliefs will be an advantage to agency since it allows agents to consider and perform actions otherwise unavailable. As positivists have seen, we cannot write a true account of the nature of rules which does not take seriously the epistemological value of rules. Many positivists have not seen how both the epistemological and other external values which rules may be meant to serve may co-habit as equals even in the institution of law. On the other hand, anti-positivists see the priorities determined by the fact that law is, *qua* law, essentially no more than a means in the service of some other end. The paradox seems to be that if rules work they do so because of the regulative and consequently strongly predictive factor which they contribute; but this part of their nature can be incompatible with their added purpose, their T, which rules also have by nature. What the positivist sees is that the regulative efficacy of rules is a fragile creature itself dependent upon agents' clear and steady knowledge of what the rules require of them. The positivist fears that if we judge rules from an external teleology, from something other than their epistemic contribution, we tend to make that contribution impossible.

This is, however, a picture, shared by both sides, which harbours a serious distortion. The tension which separates the positivists and their opponents is that which may exist between the E and T factors necessary for action. Rules being extensions of agency may also be seen as externalizations of it and we may therefore raise the matter of possible tension between E and T for an agent internally. But it is not as if we may really describe a goal, such as wanting to embarrass the government, without a large number of true beliefs being presupposed. We believe that embarrassment tends to be disliked and that therefore the government would do so; we believe that doing what they dislike causes some further law-related change in the behaviour of governments or voters; we will have some beliefs about how embarrassment may be appropriately caused; finally we believe that the embarrassment of the government, that event, is what will satisfy the desire we have. It is a well-entrenched view, in any case, that the application of any concept strictly assumes a network of supporting beliefs.[1] In the case of teleological concepts it will be more clearly the case since they have the additional complication of necessarily implying the last of the above beliefs about the relation of two events.[2]

This same tension exists between what is called 'the right' on the one hand, and 'the good' on the other.[3] 'The right' involves the basic set of values which come out of and which extend agency and which then allow us to pursue 'the good' which refers to what is identified by the best theory of our T – the best theory of goals, excluding those of agency itself. It is again the tension with agency itself, between E on one side and T on the other. Our view, for which arguments are about to be made, is that this separation is an illusion. We cannot properly separate epistemological from teleological considerations.

We may conditionally say then that E and T are not really separable. The description of a T essentially implies an E. If we take the externalization of this, which is to express it in terms of rules and goals, it would be that an R and T are not really separable.

What we want, T^1, will be an event set in circumstances and conditions – that is what is desirable. The full description of that teleological event will include or imply that setting. That description or knowledge is what defines T^1; and R, the rule meant to achieve it, states or implies those essential specifications of T^1. Hence R will be indesociable from T^1, the same being true of their internalizations, E and T.

We may now adumbrate an important and pervasive isomorphism which is to run through the remainder of this treatise but which has its origins in the concepts of action and agency. We shall in the sequel be concerned with the nature of rule-governed practices and the law in particular. We have argued that practices such as contract are a most useful way in which agency may be extended. Rules themselves are productive of agency-extension since they enhance at least the E and may also directly enhance the T and P aspects of agency. But rules may be seen as more than this: they may be seen as isomorphic to action.

Suppose that an action may be laid out as follows: We go through an exercise in choice which inextricably involves epistemological considerations and goals: we only know which event we seek – and it *is* events we seek – through their proper description. The epistemic exercise we go through propaedeutic to action is in order to *get* the right description without which the event is not identifiable. We then intend that event and our bodies perform the antecedent event which we believe will eventuate in the desired event. Sometimes, of course, these two events are identical. An action then involves E, then P and finally a T^1, one's particular goal. Rules, we are about to argue in some detail later in this chapter, being extensions of agency are, we may expect, isomorphic with actions. A rule has a deliberative antecedent which is implied by the set of circumstances – under a description – which define when the rule is properly applied; it has behaviour which is prescribed or proscribed and which is believed to eventuate in the desired event or sort of event. A rule has an E then a P and finally also a T aspect. We should notice as with action that there are E factors between the E, T and P events.

There is a third level of isomorphism which, although obvious, takes an interesting turn. Agency itself, being the set of abilities which perform, will be isomorphic to the performance. But the ETP abilities of agents will, we know, be enhanced by the practices which are its extensions. Truth-speaking will expand the E ability; contract will expand both the P ability, in that we may, for instance, engage the bodies of other agents, and also the range of T. This enhancement, which is prodigious, transforms agency. Most important, however, is the continuous manner in which T is affected (and therefore E). Not only are ends now possible through the practices which were unattainable before but ends are actually created which did not previously exist. The rights and duties which are attained with the practices of truth and proprietariness are examples of newly created events and therefore of goals. In consequence, agency is not a static notion except in form. Its scope and content, the strength of its abilities, are crafted by us. As it strengthens it becomes through the practices a more artifactual thing and a more social thing. We shall return to this topic in Chapter VII, after we have examined further the nature of the practices, the enhancers of agency, in short, rules. At that time a more detailed description of the relations between rules, action and agency will be possible.

2

A convenient point of entry into an analysis of rules is to begin where many have, which is with the relationship between rules and their goals. It may, as we have seen, be expressed as the problem which exists in the service of distinct yet necessarily related sets of goals.

One set contains the properties or virtues of practices, rules or laws themselves, and the other, the virtues which abidence by those rules is presumably meant to attain. These two sets of goals have, respectively, the following sorts of members:

(a) (i) certainty, which requires decisiveness, clarity, publicity and authority
    (ii) predictability, which requires consistency, impartiality and truth, (i) and (ii) being the epistemological contributions of rules, and
(b) the basic rights of agency (ETP) and other common interests of agents such as peace, physical and economic well-being, respect, love, security and privacy.

In this preliminary division into *a* and *b* it should be noticed that we have kept E in *both* lists. We have done this to reflect two compatible facts about knowledge. The first, the one already referred to, is that the members of the *b* list are incomprehensible without true beliefs, which they presuppose and imply. The second is the fact that the network of beliefs which teleological concepts must inhabit in order to have meaning implies the existence of relations among these beliefs. It is from these relations that prediction is possible. The existence of one event will, given these relations, be a reason for the inference to another. Rules, being regulative of behaviour, are such an index of it. Since that is the essential function of rules, E also belongs in the *a* list.

A signpost is in order here. We describe throughout this treatise the manner in which the law functions when it functions properly, or as it ought to function. The relationship between *a*- and *b*-goals is considered from that point of view. One could not deny, however, that any practice may be intentionally abused or misdirected through false beliefs. Morality, another rule-governed activity, has exactly the same susceptibility, as we argue in the final chapter. Since no such human endeavours are capable of avoiding abuse there is an uninteresting sense in which what the law is may not be what it ought to be. Barring extreme scepticism, however, abuse exists for periods of time and for isolated cases. What an agent should do under an ignorant or malicious use of any rule-governed activity when therefore remedies internal to the activity are unavailable to him we have not faced. What we do face is the question of whether with the proper function of law, where abuse of all possible types is assumed extirpated, the institution itself guarantees at least that situations isomorphic with what the improper use of law can produce may not arise within the institution. The question is whether a rule-governed activity may be described partly from its actual behaviour, partly where necessary from rational transduction, which in its results is a fiduciary extension of agency. Certainly, many have thought that the institution *itself*, excluding its abuses, was not fine-grained enough, not value-conscious enough to prevent the isomorphisms of abuse from arising within. We return now to the main line of our argument.

Competition appears to take place between our two sets of goals when the conditions which are required for the achievement of the first set produce a result which is apparently at odds with members of the second. For example, we need in the law to vest authority in someone such as a judge or jury if we are to get decisions which will be binding and which will have the power of the institution of 'the law' behind them. Occasionally, however, the use of such authority and power seems adversely to affect some of our interests of the sort contained under *b* such as freedom of action or privacy. Hence apparently if *a* then not *b*.

In such a hypothetical conflict between *a* and *b, b* might seem necessarily to take priority. However, a clear line of communion exists between *a* and *b* which makes choice more difficult. Goals of the sort found under *a* are, for the most part, embraced by us because they tend to be sufficient and necessary for the achievement of a satisfactory degree of *b*-type goals. 'Tending to be a sufficient and necessary condition for' means, first, that as a matter of fact, acts done in accordance with the objectives under *a* tend to produce the objectives under *b*; so there is a causal relation between *a* and *b*. Second, it means that there is, as a matter of fact, no other comparably successful way, given what we are and what the world is, to attain *b* other than by behaviour in accordance with *a*. For example, some of our goals such as peace and safety cannot be achieved without certainty, predictability, authority and other such *a*-type goals being characteristics in the governance of our behaviour. This relationship between some of our substantive goals, *b*, and these adverbial conditions of their achievement, *a*, we take to be a hard won fact of our sort of life.

It might appear at first that this relationship would still give *b* a clear priority over *a*, as it seemed in the above case of conflict, but actually their intimacy prevents any simple choice. It does so because the status of the members of *a* become elevated to those of *b* to the degree that *a*'s members are seen not only as a sufficient, but, in the circumstances, as a necessary condition of *b*. When the members of *a* are seen as tending to be necessary and sufficient for *b* then they tend to be seen as equal in value rather than as subordinate.

As an alternative means of making the point we may say that the description of the *a*-content of a rule – what counts as a case of consistency for example – is determined by the proper description of the *b*-content of the rule and *vice versa*. We do not and cannot separate the two. If we do, we have a description of one or the other or both which is incomplete in a fashion that may allow us to generate both acts and judgments which are informed by false beliefs. Each description without both elements, *a* and *b*, may be a false description.

An instance of this reciprocity can be seen in the workings of both contract and its informal counterpart, promising. We can assume that the substantive goal of contract and promising is to facilitate planning. Unless, however, there were some high degree of decisiveness, clarity, publicity, predictability, consistency, authoritativeness and impartiality predicable of the rules of contract themselves, planning would be undescribed. This is to say that *a* is a necessary condition for *b*. Moreover, it seems that *b* is achievable to a desired degree when *a* is in operation. This is to say that *a* is a sufficient condition for *b*. If this is true then *a* tends to be as valuable as *b* since it tends to be the unique condition of *b*; a relation of practical equivalence now exists between *a* and *b*.

If we grant that $a \longleftrightarrow b$ is true as described above, we are in possession of an extremely powerful premise. The implication is that the goal, *b*, which the law targets, has a true description which is incompatible with a goal which could be achieved *without* rule-governedness, and *vice-versa*. It is the *same* goal, alternatively described, as that goal which is achieved through rule-governedness through proceeding *a*'ly: $a \longleftrightarrow b$.

What we have to ask is what form a law must have in order for that law to include under its aegis only those cases which are consistent with the '$a \longleftrightarrow b$' relation and to avoid including those cases which are not consistent with that relation. Furthermore, the form of the law will have to be successful in achieving this demarcation whatever the particular cases are.

The important point at this stage is that in our view laws would systematically exclude from their purview those cases where formal and substantive considerations were incompatible and license only those cases where they were compatible. That would be the basic form of each law or rule.

This compatibility is maintained when a rule is viewed as including its policy or goal(s) somehow in its effective description. But because the application of a rule can lead to undesirable consequences, we must at times apparently choose either goals or rules, but not both. No system of explanation nor any science would countenance such a forced choice. No hypothesis is disjunctive in this way with its data in an explanatory system. We argue that no law is disjunctive with its policies in a legal system. Thus the policy must be included in such a way that no disjunctive choices between policy and rule are forced on the system.

Contrary to this position, most of the interesting and related disputes in the philosophy of law and other areas have assumed that one has to make disjunctive choices. For example, the disputes in law between positivists and non-positivists, the disputes regarding the relationship of 'law and morality' and 'principle and rules', and those between 'rule utilitarianism' and 'act utilitarianism' have all been disjunctive in spirit. They all come down to the question: what choice shall we make when the *desiderata* of acting according to the rule, that is acting according to our *a*-type goals, conflict with the *desiderata* of acting according to other, independent *desiderata* such as our *b*-type goals.

The assumption of a disjunctive form of the law is easily seen in 'the law versus morality' debate. In the Hart-Fuller[4] version, for instance, the question is whether a 'law' can be deemed such when it is 'immoral'. Hart wants to say 'yes' to this and thereby indicates that in the event of a choice between *a* and *b* he is for *a*, 'the law', and not *b*, its content. This implies that Hart seeks a definition of the 'law' which does not have 'morality' as a necessary condition. Fuller, on the other hand, wants 'the law' to contain morality as a necessary condition; and, furthermore, when *a* conflicts with *b*, he opts for *b* as being the determining ingredient of 'the law'. Both would agree that there are at least two possible ingredients to decisions in 'the law': the clearly demarcatable or positive 'law' or rule-governed feature and a 'moral' or goal-like feature. A Fuller-like view implies that where the law creates choices between *a* and *b*, the one with the higher value, usually *b*, must be chosen. Our claim is that the law creates no such choice.

Disjunctiveness occurs in other positivist/non-positivist debates. It appears in the debate over whether the legal rules can be thought of as a sufficient basis for legal decisions or whether some other anti-positivist ingredient such as 'principles' or 'policies' is necessary. And it appears in the works of writers[5] who claim that when we are, by circumstances, faced with a choice between observing the law itself and thereby preserving *a*-type goals, and furthering or defending 'principles' or 'policies', then the latter ought, sometimes at least, to dominate the former.

Graham Hughes[6] argues that legal decisions employ many considerations which are not rule-governed and that the outcome of a decision will often depend upon 'acceptable arguments', which have no regulated way of entering the system. To allow this is to pit *a*-type goals against others, at least on occasion. To that extent Hughes, too, is a disjunctivist. The 'Law, Science and Policy' approach of Myres McDougal and Harold Lasswell[7] and their colleagues is also disjunctive in that the *a*-type goals such as stability of expectations are considered merely as policies which can be weighed against the substantive goals when a conflict arises.

In the rule-versus-act utilitarian debate,[8] a slightly different disjunct is claimed to be allowed by the form of the law. That debate sets up a choice between either acting in accordance with the rule or law or acting in accordance with the 'utilities' of the particular case. We can, it is believed, sometimes be faced with the kind of choice which faced the 'virtuous' missionary: either he accepts from the tribe the sexual gift of a nubile native virgin or he risks certain death for himself and his party through offending the tribe.[9] The point of this example is to produce a case where a disjunctive choice between *a*- and *b*-type matters is plausible. The relevant implication of all this is that the law is viewed as having a form which allows the emergence of cases where a choice must be made between *a*- and *b*-type matters. We shall argue that this is not the case in law nor in any other rule-governed system.

3

We propose to defend our own view that the law is not disjunctive in nature by looking at the structure of some rather pedestrian practices which should, because of their similarity to the law, embody the sorts of 'disjuncts' described above (or some recognizable relative) if the disjunctive theory is true. We shall determine whether, in these everyday and informal laws and social-linguistic practices, such a disjunctive spirit is present. Our view is that it is not.

Our first step will be to outline a theory of how such practices function without this kind of apparent disjunction. We will then show that the mechanisms which are inherent in the informal laws governing our pedestrian social practices and which expressly address themselves to the disjunctions exist also in the law. Let us look closely, then, at a feature which probably all of these practices or informal laws must have. We shall call it their invocation feature.[10]

It is the nature of such social practices as promising, stating, commanding, blaming, marriage, and others that certain consequences are intended, by rule, to follow the invocation of the practice. Most, if not all, such practices take pains to distinguish clearly their invocation from the body of the practice. This separation is worthy of maintenance for very good reasons. Take the case of promising. If you say 'I promise' under certain conditions, for example in the absence of duress, that is sufficient to invoke the practice. This means that such things as your intention to do what you promised to do and your actually doing so are now both quite likely to occur, *ceteris paribus*. Consequently, your hearer has certain justifiable expectations, and you are criticizable, *ceteris paribus*, when those consequent expectations go unfulfilled.

The main point of the practice is to give the hearer some assurance that these consequents will occur, for it is only on this basis that he can plan further. (Without this assurance, the practice of promising and its like cannot be explained.) The hearer's assurance rests upon the invoking action of the speaker, upon his 'I promise'. The causal sequence which lies behind this will be dealt with shortly. We are concerned with the need for this heralding act and what its properties have to be. First, we shall deal with the need.

There must be a public, clear, dateable act on the part of the promisor which will tell the hearer that the speaker is in a certain state, the sort of state that tends to be followed by appropriate behaviour at a later time. The invoking act is *required* in order that the hearer will *know* that the speaker is in this particular kind of state. In addition, such an initiating condition must, for epistemological reasons, have the properties of being clear, public and dateable. These properties are essential for another reason. Should the speaker fail to behave as is justifiably predictable from the act of invocation, the speaker may be punished according to the practice. Where punishment is possible, clear, public dateable evidence of the abuse is best in order to avoid dispute. Because the invoking act must have these properties, one's intention to promise, for instance, could not serve as the invoking condition. And for the same reason, one's intention to mean something, even Humpty Dumpty's,[11] is not sufficient for meaning in a language. A clear, public and dateable invoking act is essential to the survival of certain practices whether they be like the practice of promising or that which allows meaning to occur in language.

Our objective is to see whether the invoking feature of a practice – an important feature of probably all informal and formal laws – behaves in the manner which our theory would predict or in a manner consonant with a disjunctive view of the form of law.

We know that when an agent voluntarily invokes a practice there is a strong tendency to let that stand as a proper invocation whether or not the body of the practice follows as it should. Thus a man is taken to have promised if he voluntarily says, 'I promise to do x', even if he does not intend to do x as he says it, just as a man is taken to have warned if he says, voluntarily, 'Look out for the x,' no matter whether there is no x in the vicinity to be looked out for. This must be the case in order for the efficacy of the invoking feature to be protected. The hearer must always assume that the speaker is invoking the practice in good faith, or it will not work. The practice or law cannot promote hearer incredulousness and survive since his uptake is essential to it. The responsibility for the sequence of events following the invocation must be on the speaker. It is much more a case of caveat speaker than caveat hearer. Furthermore, the practice offers the hearer the weapon of punishment in order to discourage speakers' abuses of the practice. All of this is to encourage the *a*-type considerations of the practice.

But what happens when these proper and entrenched *a*-type considerations, whose presence is evidenced in how carefully we arrange matters to preserve the efficacy and believability of the invoking condition, come into conflict with important *b*-type considerations? Must we not then at least, even if never before, suspend or cancel the normal rule of the invoking condition in order that proper *b*-type goals be served? Must we not, when faced with an apparent disjunction between *a* and *b*, accept not-*a*, which in this case would be to accept the suspension of the otherwise lawful fact of the invoking act? Practices do not do this. Rather, even under such circumstances, they protect the invoking act from cancellation and thus maintain compatibility between *a* and *b*-type goals. The evidence for that is as follows.

Suppose I promise to do x but find, in the interim, that something justifiably unforeseen and important has arisen whereby I am, by the rules of the practice, not required to do x. The practice says in effect that when a more important *b*-type consideration is served by my not doing x than by my doing x, then I am, by the rules of the practice itself, not required to do x even though I have so promised, even though the invoking act has been performed. The normal requirement to perform x is cancelled by the practice itself. What else is cancelled? Is the fact that I promised, the fact of the invoking act cancelled? We know that it is not because I am still held to have promised. The fact of the promise is unchanged, which is to say that the fact of the invoking act is unchanged. This means that the question of whether an invoking act has really occurred, for example whether or not one has actually promised, is left by design unclouded by trailing questions of whether or not something of a *b*-type would subsequently occur which would defeat the invoking act. The invoking condition and the act it encompasses are not defeasible in that way by subsequent events. In the practice, nothing of a *b*-type nature is allowed ever to defeat the rules of the invoking act. If the invoking act is not defeasible by the rise of *b*-type considerations then the *a*-type considerations (outlined above), which the invoking act serves, are not defeasible either by the rise of *b*-type considerations. At this juncture of a practice *a*- and *b*-type matters are not allowed to be disjunctively pitted one against the other.

Let us examine another case, that of commands. Suppose you have been commanded to do x by a superior officer. Even though doing x is adverse to our *b*-type goals, and even though you shall not, by the rule structure of commands, be required to do x, you have been commanded. The fact that you were commanded is not defeasible; the act of invocation is not cancelled although other normal eventualities of the practice are. The virtue of this is that the *a*-type considerations inherent in having an invocation condition are not cancelled. The rules surrounding the invocation and therefore the act itself remain intact and unchallenged. What does not remain intact, but is defeated in the above cases by the domination of *b*-type considerations, is the relation between the act of invocation and subsequent steps in the practice.

What these two examples show is that in at least one important area where *a*- and *b*-type considerations might clash within a practice and where the latter override the former, their compatibility is maintained by the form of the practice itself. The invocation feature is allowed to stand undefeated while its implications are cancelled. Thus the rules of the invocation are preserved. What is cancelled is the expectation of a causal relation between the invocation and the next step, but that is not part of the rules of invocation. The over-arching idea is that in these informal laws or practices where there might occur a disjunction between *a* and *b* and therefore, plausibly, the defeat of the act of invocation, compatibility of *a* and *b* is preserved by rule. We shall argue that this compatibility goes on throughout the entire structure of the rule and not just at the point of contact between the rules of invocation of the practice and certain *b*-type considerations relevant to that practice. It did not have to be this way: we might have managed our concepts so that a man would not have promised and not have warned and not have commanded under the above conditions of defeasibility.

Some practices might seem to proceed in the contrary way. For example, when certain conditions, such as the sexual consummation of a marriage, are not met the marriage may be annulled. But this does not mean that the marriage did not take place. It means, as it did in the other examples, that the normal implications from the bona fide ceremony are cancelled, not the ceremony itself. Compare this case to one where the alleged official at the ceremony is not licensed or otherwise legally empowered to officiate. Then the purported invoking act did not meet its own proper conditions; so the marriage did not take place.[12].

The compatibility thesis says that, since that part of the practice which defines the invoking rules and act does not depend upon material from the rest of the practice, the following is false: if there is a bona fide invoking act then certain other *b*-type conditions of the practice are met. This means that *b*-type considerations are not part of the criteria used to determine whether an invoking act took place. However, these *b*-type considerations are necessary conditions of the invoking act having its normal implication for the rest of the practice. When our *b*-type considerations are not met, the rule of a practice says that although the practice has indeed been invoked, its normal implication for subsequent action and responsibility is cancelled. Thus, even where *a*- and *b*-type goals apparently conflict, they can still both be maintained. The rule of invocation and the *a*-type considerations it represents are left to reign undisturbed over their proper territory; nothing which was previously an act of invocation is now not, and nothing which now is was not before. Similarly, the *b*-type goals are not disturbed. The entire decision is predictable from the previously known relations between our *a*- and *b*-type goals. We know that no rule will be instituted, that is, will be given *a*-type properties, unless it is compatible with *b*-type goals, and when the rule is not compatible with *b*-type goals that rule, by rule, will have its usual effects cancelled before damage is done to the *b* area: R*a* ↔ *b* is served.

4

We have just described how compatibility is maintained in the relations between *a*-type goals served by the invocation, and possible *b*-type goals. We shall now show how compatibility is maintained at even a more important juncture.

We assume that rules or laws are artifacts, which is to say that they are the result of purposive human endeavour, and that they are means to ends. We also assume that all teleological relations are analysable into causes and effects. This entails that the relations between rules themselves and their goals will be one of cause and effect. We have already given an indication of how this can be done in the first section by employing the '↔' concept. Let us now see how this pattern of a rule-governed practice looks when seen as a string of causes and effects.

With most, if not all, such practices and laws there is an arrangement whereby certain effects, usually conduct, are pledged, produced or, conversely, discouraged, whether these effects are present ones or future ones or both. (We shall refer to such conduct as C.) Our intentions to invoke such effects, which are part of the body of the practice, need a sign of their presence so that the presence of the initiating condition of that causal chain which takes us from agent's intention to his future behaviour can be made known to the other party or parties involved. Hence the need for the invoking condition of a practice when seen from the causal point of view.

For invoking conditions to function as signs of the presence of an agent's intention, two things must be the case. First, there must be some reasonable guarantee that when an agent has invoked a practice, the body of the practice will indeed follow, for example the other consequences integral to the practice will ensue. The only form of guarantee available is a strong causal connection between an agent's voluntary implementation of the invocation feature of the practice and his intentions and his subsequent behaviour in the fulfilment of the practice. Any practice which has invoking features or conditions and such subsequent state of affairs meant to be linked with it requires the existence of such a strong causal chain. What enables this causal relation to exist is, of course, the agent's nature, his rationality, perception of facts and consequences, tendency to act on good reasons and his susceptibility to controls and penalties: his agency. The ubiquity of this sort of agent is implied by how invoking conditions work, that is, by their causal relations to certain other states of affairs in practices. Without the existence of agents with such traits of character, practices could not successfully maintain any of their linking features.

There have existed and still exist practices which have no sufficient causal basis. Inevitably, such practices will fail. Some will persist because of the belief that there is a causal basis, some hypothetical entity which gets the job done, when actually there is no such entity in existence. Witchcraft, demonology, exorcism and healing rites are some examples.

Let us now broaden our causal analysis and look at a typical causal chain which is necessary for a practice to function. The links will run as follows.

(1) The agent, for whatever reason (causal expositions must begin somewhere) has certain goals which are either *b*-type goals themselves or are causually related to them.
(2) These goals are achievable through certain actions, C. These actions will be those either prescribed or proscribed in the practice.
(3) The knowledge of the above two links causes the normal agent to be in a mental state in which he intends to act in a way which realizes his (not necessarily egoistic) goals.
(4) The intention to produce this causal sequence with the desired final effect or goal causes the properly trained agent to give notice of his intention. That is to say, he produces a public act, often verbal, which is evidence that (3) is the case. This constitutes the invocation of the practice.

For the fourth link to occur, agents must be trained. The invoking act of the practice is not a natural event in the way in which the others are (which is why in meaning theory this sort of case is called 'non-natural' meaning);[13] we forge it ourselves in order to achieve *a*-type goals.

(5) The agent's verbal action in (4) produces in the hearer the belief or attitude that either the agent intends to do x or the agent wants the hearer to do x.
(6) In some practices, the third link tends to cause the agent to perform certain actions indicated in the second link which are intermediate or sufficient causes in achieving the goals of the practice, which in most cases are the agent's goals as described under 1. Promising and inviting would be examples of this. In other practices, the fifth link tends to cause the hearer rather than the speaker to perform certain actions or to have certain attitudes, beliefs, etc., which are causally linked to the agent's desires under clause (1). Examples are warning, commanding, insulting, stating and greeting.
(7) The *b*-type goals of the practice which are often coincidental with the agent's goals under (1) are achieved.

Clearly, the requirement that the agent's desires under (1) must be causally linked to the *b*-type goals under (7) permits only certain desires under (1).

Our supposition, then, is that for any useful rule or practice or law to come into existence, a causal chain like that described above must be firmly and naturally in existence or easily evocable in nature. Practices must be built on what can be achieved within agency. In order to achieve *b* in an *a*-type fashion, for example, in order to achieve the reduction of violence, *b*, by means of a line of action regulated with *a*-type properties, a well-entrenched causal route must be readily available to form the basis of the rule, which will take us to *b* in an *a*-like fashion. Otherwise the rule is literally without effect.

Very often the rule we select in order to take us towards *b* is one which enjoins us to do or not do C. The idea is that doing C tends to get us to *b*. Only when this is clear for a set of cases will we denominate C as important to the content of the rule. 'Shout something like "lookout!" to the hearer' is one segment of the rules of 'warning when danger is imminent'. This regulation of behaviour has incontrovertible efficacy when there is imminent danger to be averted. Moreover, it has most of its important effects whether or not danger is actually there to be averted up to the point at which the hearer might act to avoid a danger were there one, for example the effects on the hearer of a warning shout are up to that point the same in the event of either a true or false warning. The same is true in the case of describing or stating. It is this fact which makes lying and false warning possible: the hearer is brought to much the same state by the speaker's actions whether or not subsequent or previous segments of the practice have or have not occurred. So a segment of the causal mechanism may work regardless of the presence of certain other key elements necessary for the practice to achieve its final goal.

If this is true of the causal side of the rule, it restricts how we can write our rules. We cannot suspend the causal laws of nature by edict and 'cancel' the fact that if someone says 'look out!' the effect will tend to be alarm whether or not there is danger. We are, therefore, forced to let that part of the practice stand as having occurred despite the fact that the absence of a later necessary link prevents the causal chain from being completed.

We might think that we could alter the situation by doing what we can to get agents not to accept false warnings as warnings or false statements as statements. But we cannot do so. If we were to train agents to the point where they will not accept false warnings as warnings, they will also be to the point where they will not accept true warnings as warnings. So, if we tamper with the causal chain, say by using psychological extinction, so that agents will not react in normal ways when there are abuses, we inevitably tamper with the dependability of the causal chain without which the practice could not exist. This means that the causal chains which are the substrata of laws must be left pretty much inviolate. Further, in every practice or law we have secondary devices which we employ to reinforce or otherwise affect the agent's role in the causal chain which underlies the practice. These are the devices of punishment, threat, justification, attribution of responsibility and obligation, and the rest of our social machinery.

How then does all this look when put down into formal structure of a rule or practice?

Recall that:

R = a rule or a sub-rule with (tautologically) *a*-type properties;
C = events such as behaviour, attitudes, which are causes of certain goals in the schema;
b = certain substantive goals of the schema;
$\rightarrow$ = the causal relation or arrow;
$\leftrightarrow$ = the double arrow or the 'if and only if' relation.

So, if we want b_1 and we see that we must employ C_1 in order to achieve b_1, we would write $C_1 \rightarrow b_1$ to symbolize the fact that C_1 is necessary for b_1 or that 'we must employ C_1'; and we would write $C_1 \leftarrow b_1$ to symbolize the fact that C_1 is sufficient or that C_1 'achieves' b_1; put together these two give us $C \leftrightarrow b$. Suppose then that we have a goal b_1; and we know that C_1 will get us b_1 and that in the circumstances *only* C_1 will get us b_1:

$$C_1 \leftrightarrow b_1$$

We also know that in order to get C_1, we need regulations R_1 functioning upon agents in such a way as to produce conformity to C_1. The epistemology added by R_1 is part of the condition of both C_1 and b_1. This means $R_1 \leftrightarrow C_1$. Our schema will then become:

$$R_1 \leftrightarrow C_1 \leftrightarrow b_1$$

We know (1), that the relation between R_1 and C_1 (no matter how well entrenched) will, under certain conditions perhaps not specifiable now, break down in such a way that the rule does not produce the behaviour we want.

We also know (2), that a breakdown can occur between C_1 and b_1, for example between conduct and goal.

Additionally, we know (3), that on certain occasions, even with the schema at work, while getting b_1 from $R_1 \leftrightarrow C_1$, we will also get the loss of a positive value greater than the positive value of *b*, or the gain of a negative value greater than the positive value of *b*.

All these exception-generating clauses are necessary adjuncts to any rule, since no rule can, in its drafting, be guarded against all the particulars which these generalities foreshadow. Thus every rule is armed in the best way possible against ruling on particular cases in a way which runs counter to our interests, namely, by having the above three adjuncts as part of its very form. These three adjuncts, henceforth (1)-(3), comprise a statement of the *ceteris paribus* clause which all rules tacitly require. More of them in a moment.

The scheme now has the following form:

$$R_1 \leftrightarrow C_1 \leftrightarrow b_1 \text{ unless (1) or (2) or (3).}$$

Given this form of the rule there is no problem about how *b*-type goals function in the system consonant with the preservation of the *a*-type properties. If we are right about the structure of a rule or law then *b*s are part of every rule or law tacitly or explicitly. Given that rules or laws come into the system in an *a*-type fashion, for example under clear invoking-conditions, then so do the *b*s which are causally related to the conduct enjoined by the rule.

A more important point can be made, however. Any practice such as the law will be an existence-proof of a set of basic, (and therefore) agreed values. Moreover, it will presuppose an ordering of these goals when nothing is at stake – a pure ordering. We can, transcendentally, as it were, deduce such a presence. Earlier, and from another direction, we have argued that ETP is the ur-set. Other members of the basic set will stem from the fact that our individual teleologies, (T), contain greatly congruent values which we contract/negotiate to pursue. Furthermore the intrinsic nature of the basic set of values has enabled us to identify them. It was the implications of agency, however, which pointed out the membership of the ur-set. Other, even less dominant values, some of them even originally unforeseen, will emerge and will be incorporated by contract/negotiation into the law. They will most likely enter by virtue of their implications for the basic members. It is not likely that all members of the basic set have not yet been identified. Most questions about values will therefore not be either about their 'pure' ordinal position, or whether they are deservedly a member of the legal set. The main legal questions will concern rather *how* we are to order our values when conflicts arise, when other values are at stake, when the pure order is disturbed. But the pure order must be the engine with which we begin although the 'impure' order is what the law strives to establish.

We should also keep in mind the structural identity between rules and actions, an identity which is clear once we see rules as extensions of agency, as extensions of their ETP, which are also the very components of action itself. The success which action then has in relation to its goals will be the same success which rules may have in relation to theirs. This premise lies behind our further defence of rules in Chapter VI and is part of the subject matter of Chapter VII.

We can now proceed to test what we have argued is the form of a rule against actual practices within the law by looking for the practical legal analogues of the functions of clauses (1) to (3).

V

RULES AND *CETERIS PARIBUS*

1
THE SITUATIONS WHERE THE CAUSAL CONNECTION BETWEEN THE RULES AND THE PRESCRIBED BEHAVIOUR BREAKS DOWN

not $(R \leftrightarrow C)$

We will show in this chapter that sometimes the causal relations between C and R can break down. Some breaks in the causal link provide excuses and some do not. The theory we develop will show which ones do and which ones do not and why.

The causal relations between C and R are contingent in that they assume a rational agent aware of the existence of R and the value of the goals which behaviour C is meant to achieve. If these factors are not present we do not expect agents to perform C when R applies; and if they do not we do not hold them responsible. For instance, infancy or insanity excuse one from keeping a promise, obeying a moral rule, or participating in other kinds of practices where youth or mental illness renders the person incapable of understanding and acting according to the rule.

The same holds true in the law. We neither punish nor hold responsible infants[1] or mentally ill persons[2] who are unable to appreciate the nature and consequences of their acts because so doing would have no deterrent or educative effect. Infancy and insanity are effective legal defences only when their presence breaks the link between R and C. Automatism,[3] whether due to insanity or other causes, constitutes a defence in the criminal law, precisely because it prevents the existence of the causal linkage between the rules and the conduct prescribed.

Compulsion or duress is a defence for most crimes except those of a very serious nature involving harm as serious or more serious than that threatened against the agent.[4] When coercion breaks the causal link between R and C then it is pointless and counterproductive to expect compliance.

An honest[5] and reasonable[6] mistake of fact can constitute a defence when, if the accused had not been mistaken about the fact, no law would have been broken.[7] A person who honestly and reasonably believes that his spouse is dead and then remarries would not be guilty of bigamy if the belief turns out to be untrue.[8] Given the mistake of fact, there is no way that the rule can affect the behaviour, C.

Inability to comply with the practice or rule is another defence. When we cannot do C, then R will not get us C, consequently, C cannot be required. We do not, for instance, expect people to keep impossible promises or commands. Most systems of law provide that where, subsequent to the formation of a contract, circumstances arise which render the contract impossible to perform, the contract is discharged and performance is not required. In the common law this principle is known as the doctrine of frustration of contract.[9] The doctrine does not apply where the circumstances are intentionally self-induced, since requiring damages for breach of contract to be paid will prevent people from intentionally frustrating their contracts.[10] The causal relation between R and C is thus maintained. The legal maxim *lex non cogit ad impossibilia* reflects the principle referred to by Glanville Williams as 'a compelling principle of humanity and justice' that 'where the law imposes a duty to act, non-compliance with the duty will be excused where compliance is physically impossible'.[11] Where it is the accused's own actions which prevent compliance, impossibility will not be a defence since it is within the power of the accused to comply with the law by refraining from doing anything which would have prevented his compliance.

Under certain circumstances, if one of the links in the chain of cause and effect is missing, we will hold people responsible and apply a sanction when so doing is likely to restore the link. We will often apply the sanction even though a person failed to comply because he was unaware of the existence of the rule because so doing will require people to make themselves aware. Ignorance of law, for instance, is generally not a defence.

The theory will also explain the rationale behind the so-called strict liability offences. Even where a statute may appear to impose liability without fault, the common law requires that the causal relation between C and R will be present. This principle has been stated by the Privy Council as follows:[12]

> But it is not enough in their Lordships' opinion merely to label the statute as one dealing with a grave social evil and from that to infer that strict liability was intended. It is pertinent also to inquire whether putting the defendant under strict liability will assist in the enforcement of the regulations. That means that there must be something he can do, directly or indirectly, by supervision or inspection, by improvement of his business methods or by exhorting those whom he may be expected to influence or control, which will promote the observance of the regulations. Unless this is so, there is no reason in penalising him, and it cannot be inferred that the legislature imposed strict liability merely in order to find a luckless victim. . . . Where it can be shown that the imposition of strict liability would result in the prosecution and conviction of a class of persons whose conduct could not in any way affect the observance of the law, their Lordships consider that, even where the statute is dealing with a grave social evil, strict liability is not likely to be intended.

In addition to providing a theoretical basis for all of the above defences, the theory shows why certain kinds of defences will not work. It explains why, when an accused could have prevented himself from getting into a foreseeably rule-breaking situation, his being in that situation will not be accepted as a defence. Thus negligent mistake of fact[13] or voluntary drunkenness[14] do not constitute full defences.[15] The reason is that some of the elements of the causal link between R and C are still present.

The theory explains how defences such as infancy, mental illness, misrepresentation, duress, undue influence and mistake work in the law of contract. The basis of contractual liability is the voluntary creation of contractual obligations. People enter into contracts because they believe that participation in the practice will achieve desired ends. Voluntariness, therefore, lies at the heart of the causal link between the R and the C of the law of contract. Infancy and insanity can affect voluntariness by rendering persons incapable of functioning as full rational agents. A contract entered into under undue influence or duress has not been made voluntarily. Misrepresentation and mistake also can affect voluntariness and consequently responsibility where, if the true facts were known, the contract would not have been made. Where both parties to a contract no longer consider it beneficial they can agree to rescind or modify the contract. If a contracting party, in spite of one of the above factors, still desires to retain the benefit of the contract by complying with it, then the causal link between R and C will still be present. If, however, the factor which negates voluntariness also negates or changes the person's desire to maintain the contractual relationship, the foundation of the causal link will be missing. The law of contract consequently considers most contracts where voluntariness is so affected to be voidable (with some exceptions) rather than void. Because the wishes of the other contracting party are equally relevant, however, the contract will generally only be voidable where that other party through its acts affects the intentionality of its contracting partner. This would be where duress, undue influence and misrepresentation are exercised by that first party upon the second. In addition, if the first party is aware that the second is either insane or holding a relevant false belief the contract is voidable. Finally, if the first party should be aware or has not exercised reasonable care in ascertaining the competence of the second party – where the second party is, for example, an infant – the contract is again voidable. It is because of the interest of the other party that courts are reluctant to intervene in a contract where one party has been mistaken and the other party is neither responsible for or knew of the mistake.[16]

2
SITUATIONS WHERE THE CAUSAL CONNECTION BETWEEN THE PRESCRIBED CONDUCT AND THE GOAL OF THE RULE BREAKS DOWN

not (C $\leftrightarrow$ *b*)

If, under certain circumstances, compliance will clearly not achieve the goal of the rule or practice, observance is not required. It would be irrational for the situation to be otherwise. We generally do not require people to give warnings where it is obvious that taking precautions will not lessen or avoid the danger. We do not hold A to his promise to B to do C where that promise was made in order for B to attain goal *b* and it becomes evident that C will not achieve *b*. Nor do we fault a junior for disregarding a commander's express instructions and attempting to achieve the desired goal by a different method when, because of unforeseen circumstances, the goal cannot be achieved by following the instructions.

The same holds true of the law. The following opinion of Harman L.J. of the English Court of Appeal is one which most judges would probably share:[17] '. . . in a case where the reasons behind the rule do not exist I do not feel bound to apply it.' Courts generally do not apply a sanction for a failure to comply where compliance would have been pointless. And it is a clearly established principle of the law of torts that there will be no liability for damage which would have taken place regardless of whether there was a breach of legal duty.[18] For example, an employer was not held liable for damages when an employee was not provided with a safety belt when it was established that this particular employee never wore the belts when they were available.[19]

There is within the law a rule of statutory interpretation which prescribes that statutes are to be construed according to their object and intent. This rule requires statutes to be interpreted in such a way as to maintain the causal link between C and *b*. Construals which cannot maintain the link are to be rejected. Because courts have varied in their opinion as to their power to depart from the ordinary or so-called 'plain' meaning of a statute[20] the rule has many judicial formulations (not all of which are consistent).[21] Most of the formulations hold that a statute is to be construed according to the ordinary meaning and grammatical sense of the words used unless such a construction would lead to a result at variance with or repugnant to the purpose of the legislation or intent of the legislature.[22]

Almost all jurisdictions now have an Interpretation Act, and most such acts contain an authoritative formulation of this rule. The following is a typical example:[23]

> Every enactment shall be deemed remedial, and shall be given such fair, large and liberal construction and interpretation as best ensures the attainment of its objects.

The effect of this rule is to allow judges to give a sufficiently wide interpretation of statutes so that the *b* goals may always be preserved. In the case of *Tedla* v. *Ellman*,[24] for example, the plaintiffs were struck from behind by a motor vehicle proceeding in the same direction. The defendant argued that the plaintiffs were contributorily negligent in that the Vehicle and Traffic Law required pedestrians to face the oncoming traffic when forced to walk on the road. The plaintiffs argued that this would be irrational at that time of night since the traffic was extremely heavy on that side of the road, and very light on the other. The New York Court of Appeals agreed with the plaintiffs, stating:[25]

> We may assume reasonably that the Legislature directed pedestrians to keep to the left of the center of the road because that would cause them to face traffic approaching in that lane and would enable them to care for their own safety better than if the traffic approached them from the rear. We cannot assume reasonably that the Legislature intended that a statute enacted for the preservation of the life and limb of pedestrians must be observed when observance would subject them to more imminent danger. . . . The generally accepted rule and the reasons for it are set forth in the comment to section 286 of the Restatement of the Law of Torts: 'Many statutes and ordinances are so worded as apparently to express a universally obligatory rule of conduct. Such enactments, however, may in view of their purpose and spirit be properly construed as intended to apply only to ordinary situations and to be subject

> to the qualification that the conduct prohibited thereby, is not wrongful if, because of an emergency or the like, the circumstances justify an apparent disobedience to the letter of the enactment. . . . The provisions of statutes intended to codify and supplement the rules of conduct which are established by a course of judicial decision or by custom, are often construed as subject to the same limitations and exceptions as the rules which they supersede. Thus, a statute or ordinance requiring all persons to drive on the right side of the road may be construed as subject to an exception permitting travellers to drive upon the other side, if so doing is likely to prevent rather than cause the accidents which it is the purpose of the statute or ordinance to prevent.

3
SITUATIONS WHERE IN GIVEN CIRCUMSTANCES THE CAUSAL LINK WILL GIVE *b* BUT ALSO THE LOSS OF A POSITIVE VALUE GREATER THAN THE POSITIVE VALUE OF *b*, OR THE GAIN OF A NEGATIVE VALUE GREATER THAN THE POSITIVE VALUE OF *b*

(We will shorten this to '*b* and something worse than *b*', asking the reader to keep in mind that the shortened version means as set out above.)

$$C \rightarrow b \text{ and something worse than } b$$

We do not require compliance with rules or practices under circumstances where, although the conduct allows us to achieve our ends, it produces other negative effects which are sufficiently bad that it is more important to prevent them than it is to achieve the goals of the rule or practice. The practice of truth-telling, for example, *is not* absolute. Lying is not only permitted but preferred when telling the truth will produce negative results the prevention of which outweigh the value of passing on true information. If a person who intends to murder asks the whereabouts of his intended victim under circumstances where some response must be made, one would not be expected to tell the truth and would not be subject to criticism for lying. Nor would one be open to criticism for failing to give a warning when the anxiety which would result would increase the danger. Nor would a person who had been warned be expected to take precautionary measures where they would only tend to aggravate the risk warned against. The form of the rules or the practice itself provides for these exceptions.

The same corrective structure exists in the law. The world is a fairly predictable place. We can therefore meet predictable contingencies by building particular exceptions into many of our legal rules. No legislature, however, is wise enough to foresee all contingencies. Although the unforeseen does not arise that often, situations can occur where if the rule is applied under the particular circumstances, the results will run counter to our *b*-type goals. Consider the following example. An intoxicated man, walking along, sees a car which has been parked on a slope start to roll forward because the driver had forgotten to put on the emergency brakes. At the same time, he notices small children playing on the road at the bottom of the hill. He therefore jumps into the slow-moving car and is able to bring it safely to a stop before it strikes the children. If the rescuer was charged, convicted and punished for 'driving a vehicle while impaired' then the legal system would be in the position of deterring the very kind of activity which the law generally encourages.[26] On the other hand, if the law is not applied to the case, then the *a*-type goals seem to be affected since it would no longer be clear what 'when driving a vehicle while impaired' does mean if the above case is not included within its ambit.

Practically every legal system avoids this in a rule-like manner by a legal defence called the defence of necessity.[27] This defence, in essence, provides that where the harm which would be caused by complying with the law outweighs the harm which could be caused by breaking the law, and the harm cannot be avoided in any manner except by breaking the law, then the breaking of the law is justified.

Where this defence is not contained in a criminal code, as in Canada, the defence is still available as a common law defence. One of the clearest provisions is that to be found in the American Law Institute's Model Penal Code:[28]

(1) Conduct which the actor believes to be necessary to avoid a

harm or evil to himself or to another is justifiable, provided that:

(a) the harm or evil sought to be avoided by such conduct is greater than that sought to be prevented by the law defining the offense charged; and

(b) neither the Code nor other law defining the offense provides exceptions or defences dealing with the specific situation involved; and

(c) a legislative purpose to exclude the justification claimed does not otherwise plainly appear.

(2) When the actor was reckless or negligent in bringing about the situation requiring a choice of harms or evils or in appraising the necessity for his conduct, the justification afforded by this Section is unavailable in a prosecution for any offense for which recklessness or negligence, as the case may be, suffices to establish culpability.

The doctrine of necessity is an integral part of the law of torts as well as the criminal law. According to Glanville Williams, one need not go to judicial authority to support this proposition but can prove it by hypothetical cases. For example, were a surgeon to perform an operation on an unconscious victim of an accident,[29] there would be no question but that the defence of necessity would be open to the surgeon if the patient later sued for assault. As put by Sir William Scott in *The Gratitudine*, necessity 'supersedes rules'.[30] Or, as Glanville Williams[31] puts it,

> 'The Law', in a word *includes* the doctrine of necessity; the defence of necessity is an implied exception to particular rules of law.

Furthermore, a person will sometimes be *punished* for failing to comply with a legal duty even when doing so required his breaking a less important law. A captain who fails to take safety measures, such as jettisoning a cargo, and is charged with criminal negligence for causing a loss of life among his crew, could not plead as a defence that jettisoning the cargo would amount to a trespass to or conversion of someone's chattels.[32]

Sometimes unforeseen contingencies can arise which can bring the goals of two areas of the law into conflict. Such situations result in the C of one law by achieving its own b, achieving at the same time something overridingly undesirable by defeating a more important b in another area of the law. In Chapter VI, we show that the law contains higher-order anomaly-solving rules which give the priorities when the goals of two areas of the law are brought into conflict by a particular set of facts. Some instances are given below.

When a beneficiary under a will murders the testator in order to take more quickly then the end of the law of wills, which is to have the property dispersed according to the desire of the testator, comes into conflict with the end of the law of crimes, which is to deter wrongdoing.[33] If we allow the expressed intent of the testator in the will to be carried out then crime is rewarded. The higher-order anomaly-solving rule which provides that a man shall not profit from his wrong establishes the priority of the law of crimes over the law of wills. Other examples of such anomaly-solving rules are:

(a) the set of rules which void or make unenforceable all or parts of contracts to do things which are illegal or contrary to public policy;
(b) the maxim *salus populi suprema lex* – 'Regard for the public welfare is the highest law';
(c) the abuse of right principle.

4

The structural features of a law as outlined so far are instructive regarding the nature of the association between statutory law and case or precedent law, particularly regarding how a law is systematically prepared to rewrite itself in response to particular cases which run against its grain.

Suppose the law had been handed down at some time past in the form of a statute, R_1, which said that citizens were not to engage in actions which resulted in physical harm to their fellows. Obviously the goal of this, b_1, would have been to protect the physical well-being of citizens. The statute, R_1, would then have promoted b_1 by suppressing and/or encouraging certain types of actions, C_1. The full rule, we know, has the form

$$R_1 \leftrightarrow C_1 \leftrightarrow b \text{ unless (1)-(3).}$$

Suppose further that the following case occurred. Citizen_1 physically harms Citizen_2 'involuntarily' in the sense that Citizen_3 has forced Citizen_1 by 'putting a gun to his head' to commit the physically harmful act against Citizen_2. We know that the threatened results of the 'gun at the head' of Citizen_1 would unquestionably have occurred and that Citizen_1 knew this. In such circumstances we could reasonably assume that $R_1 \rightarrow C_1$ would be ineffective: we could not expect that Citizen_1 or any other citizen would be governed by the effect of R_1 upon his behaviour. Nor in the circumstances would the normally reinforcing effect of punishment or its threat make any difference. Thus $R_1 \rightarrow C_1$ breaks down. Where this occurs an exception is clearly marked and generated, and the statute R_1 becomes:

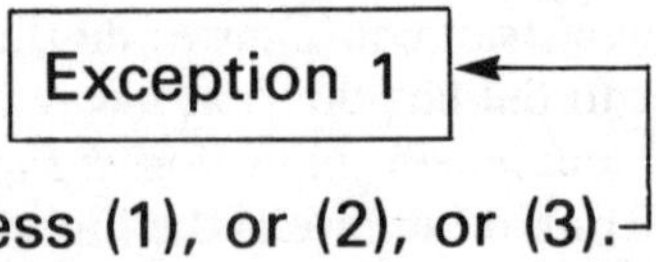

$$R_1 \rightarrow C_1 \rightarrow b_1 \text{ unless (1), or (2), or (3).}$$

In the circumstances of Exception 1, b_1 is not achievable since the requisite behaviour, C_1, is not. Therefore R_1 has no efficacy in the case of Exception 1 and does not cover it. Thus the achievability of b_1 and/or C_1 functions as criterion for determining whether a case falls under R_1 or not. This is what exception-generating clause 1 tells us.

Suppose now that on another occasion, Citizen_1 harms Citizen_2 out of 'necessity'. Had he not done so, something clearly much worse would most likely have occurred. This case plays into the waiting game and general hands of exception-generating clause 3. In that event, Exception 1 would be grafted on to R_1.

In each of the above suppositions what has happened is that R_1 is refined and rewritten by means of excluding cases which had been included in a description and understanding of R_1 contingent upon the exception-generating clauses (1)-(3) being

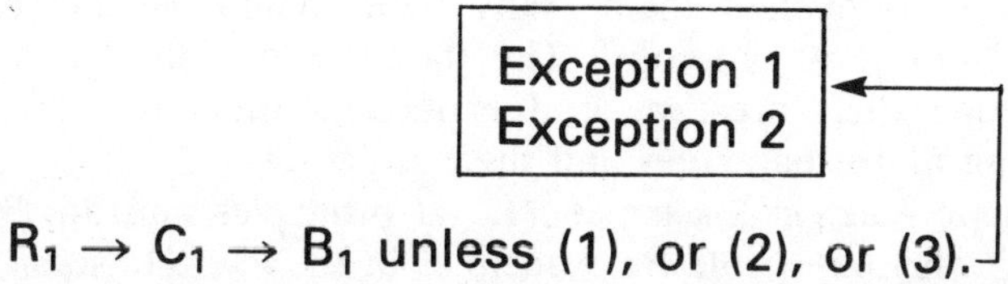

triggered. It is highly unlikely that R_1 taken alone could have been drafted originally so as to have avoided inadequacies in its description arising at some point before the unfolding world.

There are two advantages to the law being rewritten in the above systematic fashion. The first, as we have seen, is that the refinements of the rules do not overstep what is required in order to accommodate exactly the particular dissident case. We are allowed to refine R_1 in response to its exceptions as governed by clauses (1)-(3) without taking decisions on matters which could affect other unrelated cases. The establishment of an exception does not take R_1 beyond what was precisely required to establish it.

This result introduces the second main advantage of this manner of rewriting the law. That is, whatever changes must occur in the law do so in a way consonant with *a*-type goals, since it is clear to all that R_1 always had exception-generating clauses (1)-(3) as official riders.

As a last word, we might mention a criticism of the view that law can be changed within the institution of the law in a rule-governed fashion. The criticism has been cogently made by at least Hughes and Dworkin.[34] They argue that, in at least some cases of required change, 'principles' or 'maxims' such as 'A man may not profit from his own wrong' do operate in decisions (are actually 'part of the law) and yet have not themselves gained entry to the system in a rule-governed way.

The structure of the law suggested by our view of how the law gets rewritten within the law offers an obvious reply to the Hughes-Dworkin criticism: the exception-generating clause (1)-(3) give us exceptions E_1, E_2, E_3 . . . to an R_1, and as these exceptions are amassed, various generalizations and groupings present themselves to lawyer and judge. We could call this view 'Legal Nominalism' since it is the view that our Legal Maxims and Principles take shape out of case-by-case accretions to the law and are reducible to them. Nothing more seems to be required to explain them. Why then should we unnecessarily crowd our legal ontology? The theory allows us the luxury of accepting their presence and explaining them in reference to nothing more than rules and their structure.

Joseph Raz, in his paper, 'Legal principles and the limits of law',[35] also has a role for principles in the law. He sees them as 'non-legal norms' which perform, in his view, various meta-functions in the law. These include principles such as: grounds for interpreting laws, grounds for changing laws, grounds for particular exceptions to laws, and grounds for making new rules; and they were introduced in an attempt to give licence to and bring to the light of scrutiny judicial inferences which, heretofore, were buried in discretion and thus escaped the rule-governedness of the system. Probably no theorist today would disagree with the need for these functions somewhere within the law. Disagreement begins with the question of how these functions are 'grounded'. To have principles 'ground' their functions is a step above their being accomplished, as they were in some positivist views, by judicial discretion.

In our view, postulating 'principles' is an unsatisfactory attempt to achieve this. Supplying the law with premises which fill out the judicial inference patterns in an acceptable way is of little worth unless these premises are themselves invoked or introduced in a rule-like fashion and are themselves improvable and systematically addable to. Otherwise we are left with the weakness which such premises were introduced to remedy. The inferences of our courts and lawyers would now stop with these pieces of the law which themselves have neither a clear undisputed licensed entrance to the system nor a means to remedy their content when needed.

This is why we root such legal premises in the structure of the system itself. There may very well be 'principles' in the system of law, but in our view they will be generable from and 'grounded in' other more basic, licensed pieces of the system and its logic, addable to and subtractable from that systematic base, and correctable. Again, therefore, we will not have to adduce 'non-legal norms' to explain legal interference. These so-called 'non-legal' norms are generable from the legal content of our law and those other parts of its structure which we have uncovered.

5

By using the '↔' relation we have put the law into an important empirical tradition. One of the basic inferences of that tradition has the following form. Given that we have a determinate set of events, a syndrome, we can postulate a set of causes which is explanatory of that syndrome. Using this form of inference, the chemists who noticed the appearance of night blindness and skin deterioration in similar circumstances inferred that something which they called 'vitamin A' probably existed and was causally related (in this case by absence) to those symptoms. The meaning of 'vitamin A' was 'that substance, whatever it is, whose absence is the cause of night blindness and skin deterioration, etc.'. The reference was probably not known: hence, even the name given was in the form of a variable.

The meaning of 'vitamin A' was controlled by its explanandum, the thing explained. The substance which turned out to be 'vitamin A', the reference of 'vitamin A', was given to us by the world of events. Thus, while the meaning of 'vitamin A' stands in a logical relation to its explanandum, its reference stands in an empirical relation to it. We might say that while the arrow in this direction, ←, is logical (vitamin is *whatever it is* which produces the explanandum), the arrow in the other direction, →, is empirical in that we discover what the value for the variable, 'whatever', actually is, and that value produces the effect to be explained.

We suggest by our schema that the same relations hold for rules and laws. The meaning of a regulation will be controlled by its relation to the *b*-goal which it is produced to achieve ('explain'); the content of the regulation or the behaviour enjoined, its 'reference', will come from the world of events and affairs. It should be clear that on the supposition in hand the 'meaning' of the regulation, which would be 'whatever action which, *ceteris paribus*, achieves this *b*-goal', will control the content of the regulation: nothing will be allowed into the content of the regulation unless it conforms with the meaning of 'whatever it is that achieves the *b*-goal, *ceteris paribus*'. Reference here is controlled by meaning; and meaning by reference to the relation to the *b*-goal; etc.

If the content or 'reference' of a regulation is controlled in this fashion, no incompatibility emerges between our formal and substantive goals nor between our particular regulations or laws and our substantive goals just as no incompatibility can emerge between meaning and reference.

Naturally, it will be charged that such incompatibilities do emerge. We do have bad laws which are inefficacious in various ways, such as those which do not produce *b*-goals or produce anti-*b*-goals. We will be accused of having described 'the law' as we believe it ought to be rather than as it is. This will be true but inapposite. Two analogies will help show why. In providing a theory of what truth-telling is, why should we not distinguish falsity? In providing a theory of how chemists proceed in their science, why should we not distinguish their procedural mistakes? The answer is that such practices are all of them prescriptive. They tell us how we ought to proceed in order to achieve certain goals and *ipso facto* they admit of various abuses. The very concept of an 'abuse', 'error' or 'mistake' presupposes a norm or measure as to how the practice ought to have proceeded and from which there has been a departure. But, unless the distinction is made between what 'ought to be' and what 'is', the mistakes can neither be properly explained nor prevented, nor can the practice be properly managed.

We turn now from the positivist's fear that rule-governedness would be unacceptably diminished should we hold that an essential description and therefore handling of a rule must contain reference to goals. We have seen that if we understand rules as extensions of agency, as extenders of our ability to act, the E and T and P elements of rules cannot be separated. They are interdependent notions. The positivist may be seen as attempting, through rules, to devise a means of heightening the E element as if that could be done in isolation from the others. But this is to misunderstand the relation between action and knowledge. Now we direct our attention to the reciprocal view, that of the anti-positivist.

VI

THE ANTI-POSITIVIST'S FEAR

The anti-positivist's fear is that, with an insistence upon rules, our goals will tend not to be properly served or at least be in danger of disservice. This fear is fed by a certain pessimistic view of what rules are. Since we believe that rules are central not only to legality but also to the achievement of many of those very goals in whose name rules are challenged, indeed central to any ideas of choice and action, we are concerned to defend rules as capable of standing in a workable relation to goals. Otherwise they will be unconnected to action. They are as adequate teleological instruments as are actions themselves. If wanting what we do or the converse is possible in one area it is in both since they show identical resources. We intend therefore to look at a well-known and widely held position which rejects the adequacy of rules at certain points in their dealings with goals. The main portion of this chapter is taken up with showing that this view of the incompatibility of following rules and serving goals is false.

It has been argued that there are some premises clearly necessary to achieve legal conclusions and which are not rules in a legal system. Dworkin and others have called these premises, which supposedly cannot be cast in the form of rules, 'principles'.[1] Examples of a legal rule are that a will is invalid unless signed by three witnesses and that the maximum speed of a motor vehicle is 60 m.p.h. on the freeway. An example of a legal principle is that no man may profit from his own wrong. The essence of their position is that legal rules can be extended to incorporate their counter-instances as exceptions, while legal principles, also used in decisions, cannot be. If this were true then an important set of legal premises – principles – functions in an 'unruly' way.

What is at stake is that if the concept of a rule is inappropriate to certain key premises, the so-called 'principles', then agency and action are thwarted however good-minded the intention is in preserving the proper T elements through principles. We have argued that the proper T elements may only be determined in interplay with epistemological elements. Among the E elements are those derived only from the function of rules, namely those which allow us the extraordinary means of prediction of the P element and 'therefore' the E and T elements of others. We hold that a T element is incompletely determined so long as those E conditions are not yet ascribable to it. Our thesis requires then the falsity of the anti-rule position.

In assessing the logical differences between rules and principles, we will assume that rules do operate in an all-or-nothing fashion, although we have already seen in Chapter IV what this means. Their all-or-nothing fashion of application is possible only after we have agreed upon how to make precise all the concepts employed by the rule. We should, for example, have to agree upon what constituted a signature, a will, or a motor vehicle. If a witness could not sign in a normal fashion, but, say, had to have his fingerprints set to the document, that might do once we had so agreed. In addition, we shall assume that exceptions have been clearly incorporated within the rule, otherwise the rules would be of a simple categorical form and thus not very useful. The exceptions will have to be there, tacitly or otherwise. Thus, the speed-limit rule will have exceptions which show its deference to other matters, such as the use of police vehicles in emergencies. Even the rule that one ought to keep one's promises, if it may be said to be such, has exceptions allowed under the general caveat 'unless overriding and unforeseen circumstances arise'. But, clearly, having exceptions which are incorporate to the rule and having to keep concepts precise does not alter the 'all-or-nothing' capability of a maxim. If they did then no maxim could be a rule, as defined by Dworkin, or anyone.

1

Let us look now at the ways in which a legal principle is said to be unextendable, for example why counter-instances cannot be embodied as exceptions or excluded by conditions in a more extended statement of the principle. The following cases are said to exemplify the use of principles whose form is unamenable to expression as a rule. The first is *Riggs* v. *Palmer*[2] where the court applied the law that a man should not profit from his own wrong in order to bar a beneficiary from taking under the will of a testator whom he had murdered. Adverse possession, the second case, is also held not to be incorporable as an exception to this principle. Adverse possession goes as follows : 'If I trespass on your land long enough, some day I will gain a right to cross your land whenever I please.'[3] Two other matters which are claimed not to be incorporable as exceptions to the principle that a man may not profit from his own wrong are, 'If a man leaves one job, breaking a contract, to take a much higher paying job, he may have to pay damages to his first employer, but he is entitled to keep his new salary,'[4] and 'If a man jumps bail and crosses state lines to make a brilliant investment in another state, he may be sent back to jail, but he will keep his profits.'[5] We should ourselves like to add at a later point six more 'counter-instances' which proponents of this view, such as Dworkin, would have to claim were not to be captured by a more extended statement of the principle that a man shall not profit from his own wrong.

We shall now offer an extension of the principle and then show how and why this maxim operates as a rule and, further, how it requires for its own operation certain hierarchical considerations. We find these hierarchical considerations essential to legal decision, but they are integral to the system and employable in a rule-like fashion in legal decisions unlike that which is claimed for 'principles'.

In order to show that the so-called principle, 'A man may not profit from his own wrong,' actually functions as a rule, we suggest the following expansion which would allow it the claimed rule feature of 'all-or-none' application: Where it is the case that, under the existing rules of law, the doing of a wrong will allow a person to make a profit and that profit will tend to act as an inducement to do that kind of wrong, then the law shall proceed to remove that inducement. We will show that this rewrite clearly excludes the so-called counter-instances from falling under the rule and, furthermore, that it provides a systematic base from which other, as yet unforeseen, situations could be excluded. The methods of exclusion will be the same as those which are used to keep kinds of situations from inclusion with any rule: (1) by showing that the sufficient and necessary conditions of the rule do not apply to the specific example, (2) by making precise the concepts employed by the rule, and (3) by the subsequent incorporation of exceptions into the statement of the rule. If the proper extension of 'principles' can be accomplished in this way, they would thereby deserve the title of 'rule'.

One of the earliest examples of the application of the rule 'no profit from one's wrongs' was in *Fauntleroy's Case* in which the court refused to allow the assignees of an insurance policy on the life of an executed felon to collect on the grounds that if it were possible for people thus to insure themselves against one of the consequences of criminal actions in order to provide for their families, this would 'take away one of those restraints operating on the minds of men against the commission of crimes, namely, the interest we have in the welfare and prosperity of our connexions'.[6] The rule has been applied to prevent murderers taking under the will of their victim[7] or under a life insurance policy where their victim is the insured.[8] In *Cleaver* v. *Mutual Reserve Fund Life Association*, the Court of Appeal held that a wife could take no benefit from a policy of insurance on her husband whom she had murdered.[9] Lord Justice Fry, in an oft-quoted formulation of the rule, stated, 'It appears to me that no system of jurisprudence can with reason include among the rights which it enforces rights directly resulting to the person asserting them from the crime of that person.'[10] The court held, however, that it would not function to bar the children from taking as they would take through their father. The money would, therefore, have to be paid by the insurance company on the death of the father but it would go directly into his estate. In the words of Lord Esher, 'the rule of public policy is not to be carried further than is necessary to ensure the object.'[11] It has been applied where the killing of a testator is manslaughter rather than murder,[12] and it has been applied to intestacy[13] and the right of survivorship in a joint tenancy[14] where a person could gain through the wrongful causing of the death of a relative or joint tenant. Where a murderer commits suicide, the courts have not allowed the gain to go into his estate as the desire to benefit one's family can function as inducement to do a wrongful act.[15] For this reason it has been held that the personal representative of a person who commits suicide where such an act is contrary to law, cannot recover moneys payable on an insurance policy on his own life.[16]

There are other examples of the application of this rule, which involve other matters than the wrongful causing of death. 'The law will not admit the validity of an insurance which assists or encourages the insurers or assured in the commission of an unlawful act.'[17] The courts for similar reasons will not allow a person to recover as damages breach of contract losses suffered as a reparation for one's own crime.[18] Where a person wrongfully takes goods from another he must, above and beyond any other damages, pay a sum for the benefit of his usage,[19] and may be required to pay over to the rightful owner any profits he acquired through his wrongful taking.[20] If a person gains a financial advantage through an act of trespass[21] or by defaming another,[22] the courts will remove that profit in the form of punitive damages.

In each of these cases there is present the condition that the profit or gain would tend to act as an inducement to commit a wrongful act or an act which the courts consider to be against public policy. This is not to say that rules are incorrigible. They occur in systems and, as we have seen, are subject to being 'worked through' and kept compatible with other aspects of the system. One cannot defend the view that rules are all or nothing in a sense which denies this. For if it is insisted that rules are incorrigible and thus, once they are formulated, isolated from other considerations, then it will be simple to find examples of propositions which may have been mistaken for rules but are not, since then nothing will be a rule.

There are, however, a good number of other apparent counter-instances which can be raised against the principle in action. A first set of these has now been excluded as counter-instances on the grounds that although they constitute situations in which a man profits from his wrongdoing, they do not fall under the condition of the rule that the profit will tend to act as an inducement to do that kind of wrongful act. So they fail to satisfy the necessary conditions for the application of the rule.

The rule does not prevent a person from taking under a will, by intestacy, as beneficiary of a life insurance policy, or under the right of survivorship of a joint tenancy, where the cause of the killing is insanity in the taker,[23] because the taker was not induced to act wrongfully by the possibility of profiting. Similarly, the rule does not apply where the wrongful act is not intentional since only intentional acts could be said to be done for the purpose of achieving a profit. The above holds true even where the negligence is so gross as to result in a criminal conviction for manslaughter.[24]

The maxim that a man shall not profit from his own wrongs is found to be non-applicable to these cases, not because of a 'weighing factor', or other typically unruly consideration, under which it was so found but because of the irrelevance of the maxim as displayed by its rationale. Were any of the cases cited above found to be cases coming under the maxim in question, they would have been wrongly found. We do not have the option, if we understand the rule, of finding for or against in the above cases, as 'weighing' would suggest. It applies in an all-or-nothing fashion *to the degree that any rule can*. Any case holding that the maxim is a defence to an insurance company's indemnifying a policy holder for his liability as a result of his negligence is simply wrongly decided, as this would defeat the whole purpose of liability insurance in regard to motor vehicles.[25] There will, of course, as with most rules, be borderline cases, such as when the person who stands to profit from a wrong, although not legally insane, is suffering from a degree of mental illness sufficient to diminish responsibility,[26] or where the act resulting in legal liability is a mixture of negligence and intentional wrongdoing. Usually, however, if an element of intent was present, the case comes within the condition of the rule, and it is applied. In *Gray* v. *Barr*, where the court denied the plaintiff's right to indemnification under an insurance policy where he had incurred liability by threatening another with a loaded gun and then accidentally killing him in the ensuing struggle, Mr Justice Lane held that 'The logical test, in my judgment, is whether the person seeking the indemnity was guilty of deliberate, intentional and unlawful violence or threats of violence. If he was, and death resulted therefrom, however unintended the final death of the victim may have been, the court should not entertain a claim for indemnity.'[27]

Another set of purported counter-examples to the proposition that a man cannot profit from his own wrong can be excluded in another fashion, which is fully compatible with the nature of rules, namely, by making precise the concept of a profit. Such precision takes place with a view to the elimination of those ambiguities in the concept of a profit which are not relevant to the rationale of the rule. Five such examples are discussed in *Hooper* v. *Lane* by Mr Baron Bramwell, who writes as follows:[28]

> Thus, if A lends a horse to B, who uses it, and puts it in his stable, and A comes for it and B is away, and the stable locked, and A breaks it open, and takes his horse, he is liable to an action for trespass to the stable, and yet the horse could not be got back, and so A would take the advantage of his own wrong. So, though a man might be indicted at common law for a forcible entry, he could not be turned out if his title were good. So, if goods are bought on a promise of cash payment, the buyer on non-payment is subject to an action, but may avail himself of a set-off, and the goods cannot be gotten back. So, if I promise a man I will sell him more goods on credit if he pays what he already owes, and he does so, and I refuse to sell, I may retain the money. So, if I force another from a fishing ground at sea and catch fish, the fish are mine; other instances might be given.

He then concludes that the maxim means 'no one shall gain a right by his own wrong; and not that if he has a right, he shall lose it, or the power of exercising it, by a wrong done in connection with it'.[29] In other words, to regain or retain what is already yours is not to make a profit, and, therefore, these examples do not fall within the scope of the rule.

Other counter-examples purporting to show that the maxim 'no profit from one's wrongs' does not operate as a rule or in an acceptable all-or-nothing fashion can be dealt with by making more precise the concept of a wrong. These purported counter-examples are increasing one's salary by breaking a contract to take a higher-paying job, and gaining a prescriptive right through continuing acts of trespass. The law generally prohibits only those acts the doing of which it is assumed will cause harm. Breach of such prohibitions will usually result in punishment or the payment of damages. If a person is able to profit from doing wrong, he will tend to be encouraged to do so. The principle that a man shall not profit from his own wrong prevents any rule or institution of the law from making it profitable to do things which it is the policy of another area of the law to deter by the imposition of sanctions. The function of the criminal law is to prohibit harmful acts and to impose punishment as, among other reasons, a deterrent. The word 'wrong' must, therefore, be taken to include within the ambit of its meaning anything which constitutes a crime.

In the law of tort the sanction takes the form of an award of damages. The imposition of damages, however, serves at least two ends, compensation as well as deterrence. Since the deterrence of harmful acts is one of the primary functions of the law of torts, 'wrong' must be taken to include within its meaning acts which constitute a tort as well as those which constitute crimes. Deterrence and compensation are not, however, always found together. Just as in the criminal law we are concerned with deterrence but not with compensation, in other areas of the law compensation may be a primary consideration while deterrence may be of little relevance. This is precisely the situation in the law of contracts. There is no general deterrence mechanism in the law of contracts to deter people from breaking their contracts.

The payment of damages within the law of contracts is purely for purposes of compensation and not deterrence. This is reflected in the fact that (1) the rules governing the extent of recovery for loss arising from breach of contract are substantially narrower than those governing the extent of recovery in the law of tort, (2) courts will not enforce penalty clauses in contracts, (3) courts will never impose punitive damages, and (4) one is expected to make every reasonable effort to mitigate one's losses from a breach of contract on the other party's part. The possibility of having to pay damages for a breach of contract may in fact act as a deterrent but this is purely incidental. That is not the rationale or purpose for which damages are imposed in the law of contract.

There are a number of reasons why deterrence is not relevant to the law of contracts. First, there are certain kinds of contracts which the courts will specifically enforce, so deterrence is obviously irrelevant. In the case of other contracts, however, the courts will not enforce performance, but instead will allow damages to be paid because they are considered to be an adequate remedy. The reason we discourage the breaking of a contract is that the consequences may be unilaterally negative to the innocent party. When adequate reparation for the breach can be made to the innocent party by the payment of damages, there is then no reason to deny the party in breach the advantages of his breach.

There are other kinds of contracts which the courts will not specifically enforce because to do so would infringe upon fundamental values which are more important to us than being able to rely on people's commitments. Contracts of personal service are of this nature. This policy is clearly articulated in the law. For example, Lord Justice Fry in *De Francesco* v. *Barnum* stated that:[30]

> I should be very unwilling to extend decisions the effect of which is to compel persons who are not desirous of maintaining continuous personal relations with one another to continue those personal relations. I have a strong impression and a strong feeling that it is not in the interest of mankind that the rule of specific performance should be extended to such cases. I think the Courts are bound to be jealous, lest they should turn contracts of service into contracts of slavery.

In *Arthur* v. *Oakes*, the court stated the following:[31]

> But the vital question remains whether a court of equity will, under any circumstances, by injunction, prevent one individual from quitting the personal service of another? An affirmative answer to this question is not, we think, justified by any authority to which our attention has been called or of which we are aware. It would be an invasion of one's natural liberty to compel him to work for or to remain in the personal service of another. One who is placed under such constraint is in a condition of involuntary servitude – a condition which the supreme law of the land declares shall not exist within the United States, or in any place subject to their jurisdiction.

We can now see that the principle that a man shall not profit from his own wrong does not apply to Dworkin's example in which a man breaks his contract by leaving one job to take a much higher-paying one. He is allowed to retain his new salary, precisely because the threat of removal of a potential higher salary would be a means of forcing a person to remain in employment against his own wishes, and this would be contrary to the express policy of the law of contract.

The social functions of contract are better served by allowing people the option of composing their obligations rather than performing them. This option is particularly important where the costs of performance will far outweigh the amount of damages, and damages adequately compensate the innocent party. This may not be a legal option in the sense that a person can be said to have a legal privilege or right to perform or not to perform. Nevertheless, it is one which the law allows in the sense that it neither requires performance nor does it purport to punish breach. Anti-autonomists in the law would have to argue that breaking a contract is an intrinsic wrong in order to maintain this example as a counter-instance to the rule. Once, however, we are clear about why it is wrong to break contracts, we do not see breach with the payment of damages as a 'wrong', given the rationale of that practice.[32]

'Adverse possession – if I trespass on your land long enough, some day I will gain a right to cross your land whenever I please,' which was considered by Dworkin to be the 'most notorious case' of the law allowing one to profit from his own wrong, can be dealt with in a similar manner. The acts necessary to acquire a prescriptive easement are not considered by the law to be wrongs. One cannot, in the eyes of the law, get a prescriptive easement through continuing acts of trespass since the basis of a prescriptive easement is a claim of right. 'The doctrine of presciption . . . presumes that the right claimed had originated in a grant; that is to say, the law presumes the right in question at some time to have been regularly granted notwithstanding that the circumstances and documentation of the grant can no longer be discovered.'[33] To admit the act to be a trespass is to deny any right. Even the granting of permission will prevent the acquisition of an easement since the crossing of the land can no longer be considered as of right. As stated by Parke B. in *Bright* v. *Walker*:[34]

> Therefore, if the way shall appear to have been enjoyed by the claimant, not openly and in the manner that a person rightfully entitled would have used it, but by stealth as a trespasser would have done – if he shall have occasionally asked the permission of the occupier of the land – no title would be acquired, because it was not enjoyed, 'as of right'.

So, this case, too, fails to be a counter-example because the law does not grant that a trespass has occurred and thus denies that there has been a wrongful act.

The third purported counter-example, in which a person is allowed to keep the profits from a brilliant investment made after jumping bail by crossing a state line, is illustrative of a class of situations where the wrongful act is not necessary to the making of the profit in that there are available alternative methods whereby the same profit could be acquired without doing anything wrong. Since non-objectionable alternatives are easily available, allowing a person to keep the profit does not act as an inducement to others to commit the same wrong. Such examples, therefore, do not fall within the conditions of the rule. Since a person can generally conduct business through agents empowered with a power of attorney, or by mail, or telephone, or by the other party coming to where he is, the making of a profit just does not function as an inducement to jump bail. One of the clearest examples of this type of situation is where a husband insures his own life, naming his wife as beneficiary, then later murders her and commits suicide. The moment the wife is murdered, there is no beneficiary, so his estate will be enriched by the proceeds of the policy. The murderer thus profits from the killing of the wife. Courts have held, however, that as there are alternative methods of changing the beneficiary from one's wife to one's estate, the rule does not apply. As stated by one court on just such a set of facts:

> To say that the object of the murder was to accomplish what could be accomplished by the mere scratch of a pen carries its own refutation and leads to the conclusion that profit via the policy was not the object of the crime. The reason for the application of the rule failing, the rule cannot be invoked.[35]

A careful examination of the cases shows that all the examples of 'principles' ' purportedly 'unruly' function in legal decisions turn out to be cases wherein they actually function in a rule-like fashion. The counter-examples can all be dealt with by showing that they are cases which do not fall within the condition of the rule or by making precise the concepts employed by the rule.

2

The anti-rule side, including Dworkin, were misled because, among other things, they failed to notice the second-order nature of the rules which they called principles. So they missed the way in which they could be more than merely tendentious in a decision and how the second-order rule could be extended to enable it to adjudicate among first-order rules. We have seen in the previous section just how the precision of the second-order rule would take place once its anomaly-removing function among first-order rules was grasped. Let us explain this.

In the *Riggs* v. *Palmer* decision what was actually at issue was how to deal with an anomaly between the first-order laws or rules concerning taking under wills and the first-order laws or rules concerning punishment of capital offenders. As the first-order laws stand themselves, there is no way in which to remove the anomaly. We can deal with the anomaly only if the conflicting laws are orderable with respect to each other. But such ordering is possible only through a ranking of the respective goals of the conflicting laws. It is clear that the goals of wills, although *prima facie* useful, are of less consequence to us than the prevention of murder. Since this is clear, we would have little choice in making the decision that the law of wills must give way to the laws of murder when there is central conflict between them.

It is extremely important to notice, by the way, that unless we advert to the goals of the laws involved, we are not able to express the fact that there is a conflict between the laws relevant to the *Riggs* v. *Palmer* case. In fact, there is no conflict between the two sets of laws in question over the matter of whether the particularities of the *Riggs* v. *Palmer* case should come under one or the other: a man could both take under the will and be punished under the criminal law.[36] To find a conflict in the *Riggs*

v. *Palmer* case or even to express that there is one requires adversion to higher-order matters such as the goals of the first-order rules. The extent to which conflict exists between first-order rules and is resolvable within the law is the extent to which such hierarchical matters are integral to the law.

If conflict and other imperfections are resolvable within the law then the law, as an institution, must contain components necessary for that resolution. At least some of these will be second-order rules. One of our main disagreements with the proponents of 'principles' lies in what we see to be the function and nature of these second-order rules. They see them as merely guiding principles to a decision; we see them as being as binding upon the decision as first-order rules. Further arguments for this occur in the sequel. There are, however, other hierarchical and systematic components whose presence are indicated by anomalies which occur among first-order rules. However, the presence of such further components does not prevent the rule model from being productively expository of the institution of law. As we shall see when we return to this strategic matter, central cases of all rule-governed activities embody analogous hierarchical and systematic features; indeed, no rule-governed activity can proceed without them.

We suggest then that the second-order law which resolves the *Riggs* v. *Palmer* type of case is a member of a set of second-order laws and that the members of this set all have the following general form:

> When a case, C1, arises which falls clearly under Law 1, but implementation of Law 1, with respect to C1 would clearly tend to interfere with the desired consequences of Law 2, and these consequences of Law 2 are clearly more important (sic) to us than the consequences of allowing Law 1 to apply to C1 then Law 1 must lose its aegis over C1, such that C1 now falls only under Law 2.

The particular embodiment of this very general Anomaly-Resolving Rule in a case like *Riggs* v. *Palmer* would be that 'a man may not profit from his own wrong', the full form of which is: *Where it is the case that, under the existing rules of law, the doing of a wrong will allow a person to make a profit and that profit will tend to act as an inducement to do that kind of wrong, then the law shall proceed to remove that inducement.* It will be noticed that this rendition of 'a man may not profit from his own wrong' is itself a form of the standard third exception to any rule argued in Chapter IV. We may think of that set of three standard exceptions as the basis for all second-order rules.

We now proceed to substantiate our hypothesis that there is a fairly large set of second-order laws which are derivable from the Anomaly-Resolving Rule. The main function of these second-order laws, which are the *ceteris paribus* clauses of all rules, is to resolve fairly particular anomalies which have arisen, as was to be expected, among first-order laws.

The second case Dworkin used to substantiate his argument that law contains standards which do not function in an all-or-nothing fashion is *Henningsen* v. *Bloomfield Motors, Inc.*,[37] where a husband and wife brought an action for damages resulting from an accident caused by a faulty steering mechanism in the car which the husband had purchased as a gift for his wife. The purchase order form contained a standard disclaimer clause, used by all the major automobile manufacturers, to the effect that it was in lieu of all other warranties, express or implied, and which limited liability to merely replacing defective parts.

Out of a very long and complex judgment, Dworkin selects a variety of statements as examples of standards which do not function in an all-or-nothing fashion, that is to say, which do not behave as rules.[38] These statements refer to some of the 'policy considerations' which the court examined in reaching the following conclusions:

(1) The implied warranty as to merchantability is a creation of the law for the purpose of protecting the consumer and placing the cost for defective products on to the manufacturer. But:
(2) Because the disclaimer clause is industry-wide, and the ownership of a car is almost a necessity, the public has no way of avoiding these costs.
(3) If manufacturers are allowed to avoid liability for defective products by imposing these disclaimers on the purchaser, the public will be injured in that these losses will fall on their shoulders and the ends of the law for which the

implied warranty is imposed will be defeated. Therefore:
(4) The disclaimer is void on the grounds that it is contrary to public policy.

Henningsen v. *Bloomfield* is illustrative of a second-order rule to be found in a line of cases where a contract, or a part thereof, has been held to be void because it would 'tend to the injury of the public' in some way,[39] was 'contrary to the general policy of the law',[40] 'injurious to, and against the public good',[41] arose *ex turpi causa*, or is illegal. Courts have used a form of this maxim to declare void contracts to commit a crime, tort or a fraud on a third party, contracts relating to sexual immorality, contracts prejudicial to the public safety, contracts prejudicial to the administration of justice, contracts that tend to corruption in public life, contracts to defraud the revenue, to oust the jurisdiction of the courts, contracts that tend to prejudice the status of marriage, or contracts which act in restraint of trade.[42] We might state the principle behind these cases in the form of the following rule which we could call Second-Order Rule 2 (Second Order Rule 1 occurs on pages 89-90). *Where a provision of, or a whole contract is made whereby the parties agree that an act shall be done which is wrong or contrary to public policy, that provision or contract will be considered as void by the courts.*[43] The general form of this principle is as follows: Although there are *prima facie* utilities to Law 1, the laws of contract, when Law 1, as in Case C1 (*Henningsen* v. *Bloomfield*), tends to interfere with the clearly more important consequences we hope to promote with Law 2, *viz.*, the laws of consumer protection, then Law 1 will not apply in C1, but Law 2 shall. This resolution of an anomaly occurring between Law 1 (contract) and Law 2 (consumer protection) has a form identical to the form of the second-order rule which was applied in *Riggs* v. *Palmer*. Second-Order Law 2 equals Second Order Law 1 in form, for example, they both have the form of the Anomaly-Resolving Rule.

The two second-order rules of law, Second-Order Rule 1 and Second-Order Rule 2, display by their identity of form a more rarified rule which is presupposed by the law. That rule is, we have seen, the Anomaly-Resolving Rule. The two second-order rules we have so far are particularizations of it which are generated when the Anomaly-Resolving Rule is applied to the resolution of particular first-order anomalies. The Anomaly-Resolving Rule would not be found explicitly in the law, but Second-Order Rules 1 and 2 are to be so found. Where new particular second-order rules are required, the generative capacity of the Anomaly-Resolving Rule licenses their introduction by legal decision-makers.

The need for second-order rules is occasioned in various ways. In the first case of *Riggs* v. *Palmer*, the need for a second-order rule was occasioned by the creative avarice of Palmer's grandson, Elmer. His action produced an unseen crux between Law 1 and Law 2. The moment that crux comes before us, we can see its resolution as being generated under anomaly-resolving rules to yield Second-Order Rule 1. As a matter of fact, the judge in *Riggs* v. *Palmer* cites an echoing passage from Blackstone:[44]

> If there arises out of them [the laws] collaterally any absurd consequences manifestly contradictory to common reason, they are with regard to those collateral consequences void.
> '. . . where some collateral matters arise out of the general words, and happen to be unreasonable, there the judges are in decency to conclude that this consequence was not foreseen by the parliament, and therefore they are at liberty to expound the statute by equity, and only *quoad hoc* disregard it.'

The court then goes on to point out the following:[45]

> What could be more unreasonable than to suppose that it was the legislative intention in the general laws passed for the orderly, peaceable, and just devolution of property that they should have operation in favour of one who murdered his ancestor that he might speedily come into the possession of his estate? Such an intention is inconceivable. We need not, therefore, be much troubled by the general language contained in the laws. Besides, all laws as well as all contracts, may be controlled in their operation and effect by general fundamental maxims of the common law. No one shall be permitted to profit by his own fraud, or to take advantage of his own wrong, or to found any claim upon his own inequity, or to acquire property by his crime. These maxims are dictated by public policy, have their foundation in universal law administered in

> all civilized countries, and have nowhere been superseded by statutes.

These citations, we submit, are actually informal characterizations of the Anomaly-Resolving Rule, serving as a preamble in this case to the generation of Second-Order Rule 1.

We now have two cases, *Riggs* v. *Palmer*, and *Henningsen* v. *Bloomfield*, which accord with our hypothesis that there is a very general rule operating in the law, the Anomaly-Resolving Rule, which generates particular second-order rules such as Second-Order Rule 1 and Second-Order Rule 2 when anomalies occur among first-order rules.

It is obvious that novel sets of facts will occur which will disjoint the first-order law in just such ways as would be easily remedied by some particularization of the Anomaly-Resolving Rule. The Anomaly-Resolving Rule sits in the wings for just such occasions. According to our hypothesis, another such occasion is furnished by those situations where the exercise of a right of private property prevents a wider group of the general public from exercising their rights or carrying out legitimate and necessary activities. In *Dwyer* v. *Staunton*[46] the plaintiff brought an action of trespass against the defendant who crossed a part of his farm when the public highway became blocked with snow. The court held that the defendant had a right to cross the land based on the maxim *salus populi suprema lex* – 'Regard for the public welfare is the highest law.'[47] The maxim can be more precisely stated in the form of the following Second-Order Rule 3:

> Where it is the case that an action which is necessary for the safety or well-being of a section of the public comes in conflict with a right of private property, but would not be inconsistent with the property interest as a whole, the safety or well-being of the group shall take precedence over the property right of the individual.

Correlative to Dworkin's argument that such maxims as discussed above are not rules is his claim that they cannot be identified by rules of recognition as a part of any particular legal system.[48] We would suggest, however, that we can tell whether a particular second-order rule is a part of the system of law in the same way we ascertain whether a purported first-order rule of precedent is a law of any particular legal system, for example by patterns of inference which function as rules of recognition. A number of legal systems contain a legal principle often referred to as 'abuse of right'.[49] The German Code contains a provision which provides that 'The exercise of a right is forbidden if it can have no other purpose than to harm some other person.'[50] The Swiss Civil Code provides that 'every person is bound to exercise his rights and to fulfil his obligations according to the principles of good faith. The law does not protect the manifest abuse of a right.'[51]

Although the French Code contains no such provision, the principle is recognized and applied by the courts of France as a part of the law of that country. One of the leading decisions on the application of this principle is the case commonly referred to as the '*affaire Clement-Bayard*'.[52] When the Clement-Bayard Company, owners of hangars in which airships were built for the French Government, refused to purchase the adjoining land at the high price asked by the owner, the latter erected on the boundary line a number of high wooden scaffolds bristling with spikes. This made it difficult or impossible to launch airships, and when one collided with the structure and was damaged, the company brought an action. The court applied the abuse of right principle on reaching the finding that the defendant's dominant motive was the causing of harm.

This French decision immediately brings to one's mind the House of Lords' decision in *Bradford* v. *Pickles*[53] where the plaintiff municipality alleged that the defendant had sunk a well to run off the water percolating under his land in order to deprive the municipality of it and thus force them to buy his land at an exorbitant price. The application of the traditional right of private property, if applied, would lead to the anomalous situation of allowing one man to hold up a community to ransom. The abuse of right principle could have been appealed to settle the priorities in the conflict of interests between the parties. The court, however, recognized no such principle as part of the common law, but instead held that no matter how ill the motive might be, the plaintiff was entitled to exercise his legal rights.

Rules of recognition are of two basic kinds: those which specify actions by which law is created, and those which use patterns of inference such as universalizability by which new rules or new applications of old rules are derived from the existing body of the law. The former give rise to judicial fiats or legislation, while the latter produce precedents, principles and legal policies. The former are a part of the very constitution of states while the latter are presupposed by the legal system in the way it presupposes language, or in the way mathematics presupposes the principles and patterns of inference of logic. We discuss rules of recognition further in Chapter VIII.

Rules of recognition of the latter type have what we might call a generative role. The fact that Second-Order Rule 2 cannot be denied if Second-Order Rule 1 is allowed to function shows that they have an identity of form. This in turn means that the Anomaly-Resolving Rule is presupposed by the system even though we have had to deduce its presence from the nature of the open set, Second-Order Rules 1, 2, 3 . . . . If the Anomaly-Resolving Rule functions as the rule which generates new members to the series of second-order rules, then Second-Order Rule 4 could be recognized as a member if it has the form prescribed by the Anomaly-Resolving Rule in relation to a particular case of first-order rule conflict.

It is inconsistent for the court, therefore, not to rule in *Bradford* v. *Pickles* as it has in *Riggs* v. *Palmer*, *Henningsen* v. *Bloomfield* and *Dwyer* v. *Staunton*. Having resolved other anomalies which are identical in form to the *Bradford* v. *Pickles* anomaly in a certain fashion it should not have refused to resolve *Bradford* v. *Pickles* in the same fashion. There is in the law, therefore, a highly formal way for deriving a second-order rule which expresses the abuse of right principle. Actually, the laws of precedent apply as much to anomaly resolution as they do to cases under first-order rules. All of this is incidentally an argument to show that none of the second-order rules are, as Dworkin would have it, merely 'weighing considerations' in legal decisions. They share an identity of form such that rules, *viz.*, second-order rules, are applicable here in case of conflict, if they are applicable anywhere.

3

Our defence of how goals or 'principles' fare when our actions are subject to rules, rather than subject, presumably, to our choices as independent agents, has several implications. The first implication of the defence of rules is that our goals or values *are* orderable and that there exists an epistemology of this ordering. Moreover, rules, as we argue in Chapter VII and have argued earlier in Chapter IV, have the identical structural resources with which to establish what the best selection and handling of a rule is to be, as agents individually have in best deciding and choosing what they shall do. In both cases our choices and decisions are meant to be informed by true beliefs about our goals: our E is meant to help determine our T. This means again that we *can* order our goals, that choice and decision are possible and that rules can accommodate the proper treatment of goals so long as they are sensitive to what we know to be true about how our goals are related to our actions. But that *is* how rules work: rules are connected to action. To see them as insensitive to the facts of our teleology is to ignore the *ceteris paribus* clauses, or, what is equivalent, to ignore that if rules are meant to determine actions they must contain the same considerations as actions. A relevant separation between actions and their goals is, however, not conceivable, and is equally inconceivable between the proper running of rules and their goals. We expand on this theme in the next chapter.

VII

THE METAPHYSICS OF LAW

1

In order to address properly most questions which are central to our thesis we should find ourselves looking at some of the presuppositions of both agency and law. These will include those of truth, reality, self and descriptions and events. We may find that the metaphysics they support has such implications for the practice of law that certain problems might be avoided, that certain moves and attitudes in the practice of law have implications for the metaphysics and that there may have been some inconsistency between the two. But, of course, the nature of the metaphysics is itself arguable. Lawyers, we hope it is not too late to say, must not be frightened of metaphysics. It is the science of the most *basic* presuppositions of a system: it asks, what basic entities and other concepts must be presupposed as existing and operative in order for the less basic level of thought and discourse to function or to be explained?

Our enterprise here will concern itself, however, only with those metaphysical notions which any theory of law must uncover. There will, we think, be no controversy about the most basic presuppositions which we claim for law. That there may be room for controversy in their interpretation is inevitable. But many important moves within a system of law by legislators or judges will imply just such interpretive views on such basic concepts as truth, reality and self. This sort of enterprise, the metaphysical, is then just what lawyers must welcome. In order to introduce these considerations we must approach from the level of those concerns with which we have been mainly engaged.

2

We began this treatise with the concept of action, moving therefrom to agency and then to extensions of agency or rule-governed devices. Commencing with Chapter IV we have concentrated on the central nature of those devices which extend agency. We must now return to agency in order to measure whether we have in our move into the extensions, and considering the nature we attribute to rules, not bent back in upon agency in a fashion which limits it relevantly, thus turning extensions into limitations and re-opening all the old divisions between the individual and the law.

The extensions of agency we found valuable for two main reasons. The first, as we saw in Chapter III, is that the E and P abilities to act are radically extended by actions which proceed according to rules. The second, although also mentioned there, has not yet been sufficiently brought to the fore. It is that many of the most valuable goals we possess are conceivable and created only within rule-governed activities (RGAs). It is this extension of the teleology of agency and the very high quality of the goals created through RGAs that gives us the other main idea of the value of rules. RGAs will include language, communication, truth, quantification, science or knowledge, and the society of others. These activities, some of them expressed as goals, are all RGAs, and the goals or desirable actions they encompass are possible only with rules functioning through agents. The fact that many of our most important goals are rule-dependent in their very conception is a reason behind the justification of the 'Rule of Law' or 'the law of rules' in action. A more important reason, however, presents itself. In action we are interested in events as particulars.[1] An action is an event caused in a certain way. What distinguishes actions from other events is that they are produced through the operations of agency. When, therefore, we express our interest in certain goals what we intend by this is that certain particular events should occur. The manner in which we must particularize an event is with descriptions which refer to it uniquely. The event we want will have to satisfy that description, namely that it is the event which in the particular circumstances of its occurrence, its time and place, will *satisfy* the events within the agent which caused it. If goals are events which must satisfy this description then goals are events which depend for their identification upon our ability to produce the relevant beliefs of the above sort which go *into* the identifying description. This states more fully the dependence of what (events) we want upon what we know; of T upon E. But since E is a case of rule-governedness at work, any particular selection of a goal which must be made through an identifying description will be rule-dependent. Not only then are some important goals of ours, such as truth and communication, conceivable only as aspects of an RGA, but all goals, we now claim, depend for their proper identification as events upon the inevitably rule-governed concept of truth.

One more important implication emerges from the nature and conceptual pervasiveness of rule-governedness. Being an agent is itself something possible only through RGAs. An agent, we know, must, essentially, be able to reckon, to appraise the truth value of propositions, to conceptualize. We cannot perform what we call actions without these abilities; but they are all abilities to deal in rules. Being an agent or an actor is already and essentially to behave according to RGAs. The RGAs are not only extensions of agency, they are a necessary condition of it. We may imagine that some preconceptual core exists at the heart of agency; some sentient or semi-sentient, preconceptual centre, which suffers or pleasures and which may be capable of behaviour, but not capable of action until the rule-governed processes, therefore the cognitive ones of course, come into play. This is the concept of self, not to be confused with, but to be presupposed by, the concept of agency.

We may make a distinction between private and public rule-governed activities and admit that such activities as private languages, private games and other private activities are possible. But they will be of limited use and extend agency relatively little. We may say then that to be an agent *is* to be committed to the rule of law, or to the law of rules, *to the contract to contract*. To be an agent is already to be a social or practice-partaking thing, with some of the second-order contracts or rules already at work.

Ideally, now, an agent will determine and be determined by the RGAs, by the language, the knowledge, the other mutual rule-governed accords reached through socialization. In each of these, the ETP aspects will be reciprocally determined, both for the agent and the activities. The state and the law and other RGAs on the one hand, and agents on the other, if we may still so divide things, will undergo mutual determination.

The lesson is that we do not have a strictly independent idea of what agents are in separation from the RGA factors which determine them, nor a strictly independent idea of what agents reciprocally determine. Agent and society will grow or shrink together through the range of their ETP abilities. The question posed at the end of the first paragraph of this section is therefore misconceived. Agency and law ought to relate in such harmonies that the limits which agency places upon law would be the limits which law places upon itself, as we shall see. Conversely, the limits which law places upon agency would be the limits which agency would place upon itself.

We have argued earlier that for any particular action the ETP factors will also be mutually determining. Our knowledge will determine the goals and the physical event meant to produce it, and *vice versa*, for each ingredient. Nevertheless, these harmonic processes are capable of being abused. When laws are passed enjoining actions which ignore the reciprocity in which our descriptions of the ETP factors must be kept, damaging consequences which would have been avoidable may result. If we pass laws which empower Boards to apply regulations without regard for other situations or other goals we have selected a goal and frozen its description under a set of facts which are not open to further determination and adjustment. We would then have not allowed the ETP factors to be eventually (sic) determining of the actions implied by the rule. Where this is allowed to happen we may neither act as agents nor as proper legislators. Each law must be allowed to enter the full economy, or theory, of all our choices and therefore abilities if it is to enjoin behaviour worthy of the name of action.

If we express this in terms from Chapter IV the regulation must transitively determine, (→), the conduct, (→), the goal, (→), the matrix.

Further, we can see that the principle of the supremacy of

parliament is obviously unable to offer what is required for law to be properly determined. We need, as others have seen, more than a bare rule of recognition for law. How could actions be properly undertaken where only one dimension – the certainty – of even the epistemological requirement is met?

Parliament, we must recall, is merely one form in which the negotiation/contract practice, necessary as an extension of agency into the foreseeably troubled waters of conflict among agents, may become instantiated. Although a parliament or congress of representatives functioning properly will determine agency, as will any other practice which extends the basic abilities of agency, this description of the relationship is incomplete. To now, we have drawn attention to the fact that agency finds itself determined by certain essential RGAs; in the next section we look at ways in which the converse is true. The fact that the relation of determination between agent and parliament, or other expressions of the N/C practice, is symmetrical is what makes the idea of the supremacy of a congress an incomplete perception.

3

We must think of the law as a body of knowledge; it is the source of premises for certain unresolved practical syllogisms, certain unresolved questions about what we are to do, and is as well the repository of existing still-workable answers to earlier questions about action. Since it is fashioned to answer questions concerning what we ought to do it will model itself upon action: the formal considerations of action will be the formal considerations of law. E, T and P will occur as essential elements in law. If, then, we take $R \leftrightarrow C \leftrightarrow b$ as the schema of a law we should be able to construe that notation in terms of the notation for agency. The matchings are clear. C and P go together as the behaviour which is to be productive of the end; *b* and T are the teleological features, *b* being the goal of an action, while T is the teleological capacity of agency. The occurrence of *b* then is a case of the capacity fulfilled, a goal had, a desire or want felt or otherwise identified. Next, R is the declaration of a rule and matches the intending of an action. Put in terms of action, a declaration, R, would mean first that the E and T features were implied; the agent wants something, (T_1), and believes, (E_1), that this behavioural event of his body, (P_1), will produce it, and consequently intends or declares P_1, which is the analogue of the declaration of R.

The schema, however, is not yet complete. The declaration of R serves an epistemic purpose which is to make clear what it is that is to be done, and by whose authority. It matches the state of intending on this score: they are both the invoking conditions of their analogous but respective practices. But this does not tell us how the rule was arrived at. If the rule is to folow the requirements laid down for action, as we have seen it must, true relevant beliefs will have to have gone into its production. A main source of relevant true beliefs will come from previous successful actions and what such actions must themselves have presupposed as true. Complementarily, the *ceteris paribus* clauses also imply the existence of such a body of truths whose members are relevant to decisions about rules and actions. We may refer, as we have earlier, to this implied body of knowledge as a matrix of beliefs, intending by that that the constituent beliefs stand in complex ongoing relations to one another. This complex of relations, we deduce, must supply us with at least many of the true relevant beliefs we employ in deciding what we are to do in a particular area, and therefore what R we are to write or declare. Some such source of true beliefs must exist if laws or rules are able to supply true answers to questions about what we are to do. This matrix may not supply all the relevant true beliefs needed for a decision on an action, or a rule, since other areas of knowledge, which are independent to some degree, will exist, functioning however on the same general action model. All truths which are relevant must nevertheless be employed; so other areas of knowledge will be subsumable or accessable by the matrix we envision. As a matter of fact the law functions in just this way, insisting on access to relevant truths from whatever area of expertise.

We may, therefore, write the action-rule scheme as $R \leftrightarrow C \leftrightarrow b \leftrightarrow M$. This shows that there is mutual determination not only between the content of the rule declared and the conduct and the goal prescribed but also with a body of knowledge, M, which is the repository of most of the determining relevant true beliefs. We may, in order to reflect more properly the order of things, re-write the scheme as: M ↔ *b* ↔ R ↔ C.

The matrix will be a rich source of inference for jurists. We can infer, for example, from the existence of the law of torts that certain values such as prevention of physical harm take precedence over freedom of action. We can infer from the existence of the law of defamation that protection of reputation takes priority over freedom of communication. We can infer from the fact that truth is a complete defence to an action in defamation that truth is more important than protection of reputation. We can infer from the defence of absolute privilege whereby utterances in particular circumstances give rise to no liability even though they are false and defamatory that freedom of communication is essential for certain activities such as adjudication in courts of law or law-making in legislatures, and that in these circumstances freedom of communication is more important than reputation. This is because it is instrumental to achieving goals such as truth which is higher in the stable ordering than is reputation or the goals to which reputation might be an instrument. We can infer from the defence of qualified privilege that in regard to many relationships such as that of employer-employee, or in regard to the activities of various associations such as clubs, businesses, or municipal councils, while freedom of communication is more important than protection of reputation, complete or unlimited freedom is not necessary for the proper function of the relationship or activities. Communications which are not relevant or which extend to a wider audience than is necessary are not protected. Thus, the ordering of the goals of freedom of communication and protection of reputation reverses back and forth according to the priority of other goals to which they are causally related.

Just as each cause of action reflects an ordering of goals, each defence to that cause of action reflects a reversal of the ordering under the conditions which give rise to the defence because those conditions bring into play further goals of a higher priority. We can infer from the existence of the tort of trespass to land that a set of goals related to the privacy possible through exclusive access to a space is given a higher priority by the law than complete freedom of movement. If, however, the public highway is blocked and physical well-being is at stake, the defence of necessity will apply. Thus freedom of movement takes priority over privacy of space when life or health is in jeopardy.[2] The existence of the torts of assault, battery and false imprisonment attest to the priority of the goals of protection of physical well-being and liberty over the range of goals sought by activity which would constitute the torts. Wherever the defence of justification functions, however, other goals, such as law enforcement and the apprehension of criminals, is given an even higher priority. The fact that no court would ever find a rescuer of a would-be-suicide liable for an assault in preventing the self-destruction of the plaintiff, reflects the fact that the law places a higher priority on the preservation of life over the causing of minor harm or freedom of choice.

Contained further within this matrix or truth-giving machine we know are the following. First there are the considerations of agency, ETP, which are paramount and accordingly protected, including the extensions. In addition, the principles which do the work of the *ceteris paribus* clauses will be included. Wherever we are, by an R, enjoined to cause C, where C will not cause *b*, or where R will not cause C, or where R will in causing *b* through C, also cause something worse than the good of *b*, the intention declared through R is misguided. In these cases the matrix will show that R in enjoining the production of such effects is forced by false beliefs. It is in these circumstances false that C will cause *b*, false that R will cause C *and false that in these circumstances* b *is what we want.*

Since R is a declaration of what we are to do or not to do over a period of time, when we discover that the contents of the declaration are in certain circumstances *not* determined by relevant true beliefs, which is to say, they are determined by false beliefs, or by non-rational causes, we reform the declaration to accommodate the purposes for which it was declared. This parallels how we act when we discover that an action we have intended was under certain circumstances subject to accident or mistake. On the next performance we accommodate the relevant aspect whether it be C, b, M or R. Declarations of rules, then, being the registration of an intention to behave uniformly over a period of time, will be capable of proper accommodation only in a case-by-case fashion. The precedents and statutes which exist will only in that way be sensitive enough to the matrix – to true relevant beliefs – to be considered as enjoinders on what we either ought or want to do.

If law is not considered as an analogue of action in the above respect, it must be thought of as enjoining what we, perforce, must do. Since this is not to be thought of as the ideal, we accept that the ongoing accommodation of rules is necessary.

It is just this accommodation which shows one of the main ways in which agents determine law. It is their actions in *actual* and various circumstances which when brought into consideration will determine the exceptions to a rule. Each rule will be open to the full range of relevant true beliefs which agents may bring before courts. Since it is agents who are 'on the ground' as it were, they will often be the source of new relevant true beliefs, or the falsification of others which are at present improper determinants of parts of the action-rule schema. Agents then are proper determinants of laws and other rules through the fact that relevant truths are determinants. So long as we continue to consider agents as contributors to truth, agents will continue to be part of the bilateral process of how we decide what we ought, by law, to do.

A law may give us a description of a set of proscribed events. Thus, for example, the tort of malicious prosecution is identified as:

(a) The initiating of criminal proceedings which
(b) are terminated in favour of the plaintiff, and
(c) are brought with malice, and
(d) without reasonable and probable cause.

This means that those events or actions are proscribed which are the cause of a criminal proceeding which caused a verdict in favour of the initiator and which act itself was caused by malice but had no reasonable or probable cause. This causal pattern into which the proscribed event is set identifies a set of events by means of a complicated description. But the agent may not know that the event which he knows under the description 'the telephone call I am about to make to the police' is actually an event identified by the (a) part of the above description: is that telephone call also an initiator of criminal proceedings?

In order 'to know the law' then, an agent must know whether the particular description, which will be a member of an infinite set under which the event may be known to him, has the same extension or reference as the event under its legal description. 'To know the law' then requires a cognitive act for which the law itself – through the descriptions it supplies – cannot provide closure. The cognitive contribution of the agent is a necessary condition for the completeness of any law.

The cognitive act of seeing that the description under which he may know an event is also that event selected by a legal description, is unavoidable in the full process of law or rules and must be left to the agent. This dependency upon agents cannot be much ameliorated. The provision of lists of descriptions in bills under which the targeted legal events may come can be of some use to agents in making their identifications, but often, as seen in regulations for example, adds unnecessary complexity and obscurity.[3] Such lists often merely get in the way of the requisite cognitive act. Unfortunately, laws sometimes insist that a list of descriptions of the type of event targeted is to actually determine the set, that only when those set descriptions are met are the targeted events the case. If we treat a set of descriptions as constitutive of a set of events we misunderstand the relationship between description and event. Given the nature of our concepts of reality and truth and their involvement with law and action, descriptions cannot be constitutive of events since reality and truth imply something regulative beyond any set of descriptions. They imply something about which the descriptions, although different in what they are as descriptions – different in meaning – nevertheless are all true of. Not even so-called policy or practical considerations should therefore require us to treat a certain set of descriptions as constitutive.

The cognition of agents, needs, to be sure, some guidance by the descriptions which law supplies but it is misguided to attempt to supplant that cognitive process with law. This tendency to test a set of descriptions as constitutive of the events or reality intended has the inconsistent effect of excluding those same events when they are described in a way which the law has not recognized has the same reference. The use of explicit regulations which identify events with an 'if and only if' rigidity is to be avoided as the most blatant expression of this tendency.

In the case of malicious prosecution the list of descriptions may be capable of supporting an 'if and only if' relation with the events the list intends since the causal patterns included in the list protect its completeness. But it gains completion at the expense of specificity which, as we have seen, is a different problem than that created by a list of specific descriptions for which completeness is claimed.

We come back again then to the cognitive abilities of the agent which must be made room for in the law if it is to function with regard to truth and reality.[4] What the agent comes to understand or know, which is the identity in reference between a given description and another, is an ineliminable part of the legal process itself.

4

We have seen that a concept of truth is essential if we are to engage in standard or effective action. Truth will, we have also seen, then be necessary to the production of propositions or rules which enjoin us to act in certain ways if these ways are to be effective. But the concept of truth has itself a semantic implication, a topic, or referent, or aboutness, as it were, which is signalled 'to be the case' when we claim a proposition has a positive truth-value. Whatever theory we have about that semantic component – some have called it reality and some today believe science to be that which pretty literally 'creates' reality[5] – it is clear that such a component is implied.

The main indicator of the presence of a semantic component is that our proposition and beliefs will be true when and only when the relevant fact of that semantic component is the case. We clearly want our laws to be true; that is, we want it to be true that what we require to be done will be the best thing to do or the thing we want done in the circumstances. Otherwise, as we have seen, a legal edict, which is the analogue of an intention, is not joined to action. If it is, however, implied that laws are true then the semantic stratum comes into play. The legal proposition or belief will be true if and only if certain states of affairs are true. Each legal edict then will depend for its truth upon whether it would be the case that what it enjoins is the best thing or the wanted thing in the circumstances. That is the semantic state of affairs implied by the legal proposition. But we know only by reference that such a state of affairs inheres from the presence of certain other states of affairs. The truth of a proposition will be capable of being caused by a myriad of unpredictable but related other truths. With legal propositions we characteristically depend upon related propositions from which to infer the truth of others and we must therefore be sensitive to the fact that what works as a prediction at one time may not at another.

The doctrine of precedent is just our way – and not only in law – of dealing with our inability to know beforehand all of the truths which will make another proposition true or false. Unpredictability in the application of law stems from this ineradicable unpredictability in inferential knowledge which in turn we attribute to the opacity of reality. A doctrine of case-by-case adjustment to that reality is our only means of coping so long as we maintain our notion of truth. None of the above is incompatible with the possibility that even our notions of truth and reality are themselves determined as well as determining notions.

On the other side of the equation to law, where we have the agent, a symmetrical account unfolds. We have claimed that the concept of a proposition implies that of truth and therefore that of reality and the consequent unpredictability of the existence of a given state of affairs from the existence of any number of related other states of affairs to which the doctrine of adjustment to truth by new precedent is our accommodation. On the side of agency we see the concepts of E, T and P where E and P are in the service of T. T has a content which is implied by our propositions about interests, wants, desires and needs, those felt things which constitute our inner life and motivants. What makes our propositions and beliefs about agents' interests true is the existence of certain inner experiences. To say that an agent has a right is to say that a certain part of his inner life is to be protected from or served by the actions of others. The reality which establishes the truth of objective propositions is matched by a reality which establishes the truth of subjective ones. Propositions about rights are then propositions which imply the existence and importance of a certain inner life. So long as we retain the discourse of rights and truth we imply the existence of states of affairs which are *both* inner and outer and to which corresponding beliefs are tied when they deserve the epithets 'a truth' and 'a right'.

When we speak then of the mutual determination between agency and law we find the idea of a core self (not yet an agent), at one end, and of an objective reality at the other. It is the ineluctability of what is referred to by these two notions which anchors each end of the schema. It is these poles which we strive to accommodate: the poles of self and reality, which includes the reality of others.

5

The question remains of the possible incompatibility between what an agent is and justifiably wants and what he is required to do by an RGA such as the law. Our view is that this question is to be phrased as the possible incompatibility between the RGAs which define an agents' interest and actions and the RGA which defines the interest and actions of the law. Let us suppose that at least part of what defines the latter is the interest in the settlement of conflicting interests among agents. Law may perhaps legitimately deal with co-operative interests as well, but since our concern is with the possible justifiable *in*compatibility between an agent and the law, the assumption which tends more strongly towards incompatibility suits us.

Clearly, where incompatibility between the interests of agents are actual, and ineluctable, solutions do not exist. Ineluctable incompatibilities may run the gamut from zero-sum types to cases where each party comes out equal in result but with less than either wants. But we cannot blame the solution for what is in the nature of the case insoluble. Whatever ineluctable incompatibility exists between the interests of agents, as, for example, between landlord and tenant, cannot be used to attack the *means* we employ to ameliorate as far as possible the consequences of the difficulty. So long as the means are identical in form to those which they, individually, would employ as *agents* in deciding a matter for themselves, they cannot alienate themselves from the activity.

The activity which deals with incompatible interests will be subject to the conditions of agency described in Chapter III. Cases of incompatibility require that ETP and the extensions of agency remain protected as much as possible. This means that the RGAs which define agency will dominate where possible. Where this is not possible and the incompatibility impacts directly upon agency itself – where rights are in conflict – then we must look at the ranking of the features of agency themselves. But that will not take us far.

First, where a particular interest, T_1, is at stake in competition with T itself, that is where T_1 is a disjunct with the exercise of the teleological ability in some dispositional way, clearly T dominates. Epistemology or the ability to gain true beliefs is not dominated by any of the others and may dominate P, except where P is necessary for E. Since E, T and P are so interrelated that the reduction of one causes the reduction of the others and certainly causes the reduction of their product in which the final accounting must be made, a simple even *prima facie* ranking is neither possible nor of use. Again we find that a detailed, fine-grained, matrix of propositions is what is required to describe which events cause more and which less protection and reduction of agency.

Of the incompatibility between agents and the law we may say that none may exist where law functions properly any more than it may exist between an agent and his decisions where they are made properly. Incompatibilities may exist, naturally, among agents, but they are not to be confused with the relation of agent and law. Agents may find themselves dissatisfied with the decision of law in such cases but that is the analogue of their dissatisfaction with what they may as agent do in the world even when they are unconstrained by law. Incompatibilities with other agents is our lot and what we may do about them a source of disappointment. Other impediments whose source may be in the external world or in us, and what we may do about them, are equally a source of disappointment. The gap which our disappointment registers is between what we may wish and what is possible, not between us and what we ideally do, given the states of affairs with which we have to work. Actually if we insist on the alienation between individual agency and the law we deny ourselves the only resource we have with which to ameliorate what the world brings us. That resource is the function of ETP and its extensions and what that implies for action. When what the world brings us is conflict of interests between agents the only way in which ETP may function is through the practice of contract with negotiation. We might, of course, fight but without rules; sometimes this would be the best course. But then we would, *ex hypothesi*, be exerting a limited agency, that limitation forced upon us by necessity.

6

It would help to work through some examples and some possible abuses of the pervasive principle of mutual determination as it is now informed by its metaphysics. The ideas of agency and what agents are required to do, are, we hold, mutually determined. Thus, the range through which the ETP abilities are to function and the requirements which law places upon this range of functions are mutually determined. Furthermore, we must remember that this is so for the reason that the requirements are justifiable as extenders of agency, and agency is itself a composite of such practices. Agency and the legal concept of negligence, for example, would then be related in that mutually sympathetic way. Negligence is the notion that we are criticizable for those acts in the commission of which we have not exercised enough care in the application of our E and P abilities. Where the function of our choice mechanism itself it criticizable, it is a matter again of the E ability being used below a certain capacity. Otherwise, our choices, as we saw in Chapter I, are non-criticizable since they are exculpatable through being involuntary. What negligence focuses on is the low level of performance of our E and P abilities. It focuses on *how* the act was conceived or performed; it does not refer critically to *what* was done, although a separate criticism of what was done is not precluded by one of *how*. The latter is the criticism of negligence, the former a criticism of the choice itself, of a certain aspect of the function of T, not directly of E or P.

Behind this part of the notion of negligence is another, that of harm. It is when our E and P abilities are exercised at a level which can be seen to leave us, or another, subject to harm that we may charge an agent with negligence. The reason we are concerned by a low level of E and P performance is because that leaves us open to harm.

But the scope of the concept of harm must be determined. That determination may be abused in two ways. They are that the considerations which inform the concept of harm overdetermine the concept of agency, or *vice versa*. Where we allow the exercise of our ETP abilities to overdetermine the concept of harm we end up with licence and an extremely undernourished idea of harm. In that case we are allowing our actions, in the extremity, to be conceived and executed without any regard to true beliefs about, or attention to, consequences upon others. Unless some adequate measure of E and P are required in that direction, we would find everyone's agency affected. This is to underline the point that the requirement of certain rules extends agency: in this case the rule is that the E and P abilities must function to a certain minimum in the preconception of an act. So an undernourished concept of harm, which may result from an overdetermination of harm by considerations from agency, operates itself with an undernourished concept of agency; it ignores the mutuality of the concepts of harm and agency.

Similarly, the concept of harm may be misused or misunderstood so that it is used to overdetermine and unbalance agency. We might have a concept of harm defined as 'any ill effect which is the consequence upon an agent of an action'. That definition of harm would not be sufficiently informed by agency. It would include not only a requirement that the E and P abilities must be exercised in the preconception of an action to a level which reasonably minimizes the chances of consequential harm – the *how* – it also includes a stricture on *what* we may choose to do. If we choose to sell a possession the known consequence of which is to lower, even irreversibly, the amount another may get for his, the above idea of harm could be invoked. Such a distended idea of harm makes it negligent not only if we do not use our E and P abilities to protect others from the ill-effects of the consequences of our actions, it also requires that in the selection of our objectives themselves we consider the interests of others. It requires that the interests of others *determine* our choices in areas of such conflict of interest. But this is unsatisfactory unless we give no independent content at all to the notion of self as opposed to others. Since we do, the interests of the self must have some impact on the conception we employ of harm and wrongdoing and must therefore to some extent be impervious to determination by the interest of others when there is such logical contrariness to the choice.

If my choices are *determined* by your interests in such contrary cases then we have lost our grip on the distinction between what particularizes agents, our grip upon their individual consciousness. To have my choices determined by your interests is to require actions of me which do not come out of whatever my individuality is. That distended conception of wrongdoing or harm finally comes from a too-narrow or disappearing notion of the self which is at the core of agency.

If we are to distinguish between ourselves and others at all we must go on to distinguish between serving one's interests despite the negative effect on the interests of others and malfeasance, between the *care* of another and the prevention of certain harms.[6] The independent core concept of a self will function as one term in the mutual determination of agents and law, even though the agency is already such a blend itself.

The law of negligence has historically shifted from a too narrow to a too distended concept of harm. Prior to, and even for some time after the 1932 decision of the House of Lords in *Donoghue* v. *Stevenson*,[7] the law licensed by its failure to impose a standard of care the causing of physical harm to persons or property in situations where the negligent act which caused the harm to the plaintiff also constituted a breach of contract to someone else.[8] This represents a failure in legal reasoning as the existence of a contract between the defendant and someone else furnishes no reason for creating an exception to the general principle that people must pursue their own interests without causing unjustified physical harm to the persons or property of others.

In recent years, the law has over-corrected by introducing an interpretation of *Donoghue* v. *Stevenson* which in its application broadens harm to include pure economic loss as well as nonfeasance. The new principle has become known as the *prima facie* duty of care doctrine and is stated as follows:[9]

> The position has now been reached that in order to establish that a duty of care arises in a particular situation, it is not necessary to bring the facts of that situation within those of previous situations in which a duty of care has been held to

> exist. Rather the question has to be approached in two stages. First one has to ask whether, as between the alleged wrongdoer and the person who has suffered damage there is sufficient relationship of proximity of neighbourhood such that, in the reasonable contemplation of the former, carelessness on his part may be likely to cause damage to the latter – in which case a *prime facie* duty of care arises. Secondly, if the first question is answered affirmatively, it is necessary to consider whether there are any considerations which ought to negative, or reduce or limit the scope of the duty or the class of person to whom it is owed or the damages to which a breach of it may give rise. . . .

The concept of damage or harm which this passage employs projects a general duty of care upon agents. Where an agent in the pursuit of his otherwise acceptable goals either unintentionally or intentionally inflicts, for example, a pure economic loss upon another then he may be deemed, subject only to foreseeability, to have acted with carelessness. This means that the agent is *required* to take into account, as he reckons his own interests and possible actions, how his otherwise benign actions – no physical harm or property damage – will affect the interests of another. This standard of care is so expanded as to become a standard of care *for* another. But we must leave some room for the concept of selfness at the centre of agency which does not require an equality of concern or care by one self for another. That self should then so determine law that law will not require equal concern and care from the actions of an agent for *all* the interests of another. But that is what pure economic loss treated as harm implies.[10]

What we must not do then is so construe our concepts of harm and interest that we leave insufficient room for the concept of an *individual* agent, one's self. This is, however, what we do when we require that his choices be overdetermined by their effects upon the interests of others. Either *some* room must be left for some of his choices irrespective of their consequences upon others or we abandon the notion of an individual agent, the individual self being too much determined by others. That should be prevented by the recognition of what the self is.

VIII

THE AUTONOMY OF LAW

In this concluding chapter we consider again, particularly in the light of Chapter VI, the autonomy of the law in relation to morality, that is, to a rule-governed system which specializes in interpersonal values. This topic will require us to consider the nature of a rule of recognition which, since at least Hart, has been an important (for him crucial) factor in the matter of legal autonomy. Those in favour of legal autonomy have held that through the exercise of rules of recognition the law may embrace any moral consideration necessary to its effective and persuasive function. This side has never denied, or at least has not had to deny, that moral ingredients must appear in the law. What is in dispute is how that set of premises with their systematic insistencies may enter the consideration of the law while it still preserves its autonomy. Hart refuses the '*invitation* to revise our conception of what a rule is. . .' by including 'in the "rule" the various aims and policies. . .' because, he states, 'everything we have learned about the judicial process can be expressed in other less mysterious ways.'[1] The other side has held that a rule of recognition could not exist which would allow 'principles', or rights, or 'the moral ingredient', a systematic and therefore ruled entry into the legal system. Dworkin is a recent example of someone who holds this view. It is not entirely clear why he does, but some construals are possible.

1

The main argument seems to be that (moral) principles expressing rights are not capable of being expressed as rules but have a 'relative weight' which is gleaned from consideration of 'shifting, developing and interacting standards (themselves principles rather than rules) about institutional responsibility, statutory interpretation, the persuasive force of various sorts of precedent, the relation of all these to contemporary moral practices and hosts [sic] of other standards'. We could not, therefore, the argument concludes, 'devise any formula, "any rule of recognition", for *testing* [our italics] how much weight and what kind of institutional support is necessary to make a principle a legal principle, still less to fix its weight at a particular order of magnitude'.[2]

This whole line fails, of course, if principles can be expressed and treated as rules, a capability we have argued for in Chapter VI. But this is not fully satisfactory since there are two misconceptions at work here. One must not only argue against Dworkin's misunderstanding of what a rule is but against his misconception of a rule of recognition.

Dworkin holds that only because rules are 'all or nothing' in form can they be recognized by rule. This is a *non-sequitur*. The fact that a rule of recognition is in place tells us nothing about the nature of the objects which the rule of recognition covers. We could have a rule of recognition which said that we will recognize as legal whatever King Ambiguous 'decides'. This rule of recognition would not in any way determine what sort of edicts King Ambiguous would hand down. It would tell us only that King Ambiguous's words are to be taken as the law; it is not meant to give us a means of construing or applying his words. A rule of recognition is not a formula for hermeneutics. We have other devices for that which perhaps presuppose other rules of recognition. Thus, 'a man may not profit from his own wrong', or 'treat all citizens with equal respect and dignity', are propositions which, even were they not formulable as rules, would be capable of being the subjects of rules of recognition. The rule of recognition when applied to these cases says, 'accept these propositions as content, however far or near they may leave you from understanding.' Other rules of recognition may now come into play – rules of meaning in this case – to help us with our construals.

Of course principles *are* formulable as rules although, as with any rule, that requires that they become, as we have argued, part of the system. It is, as we have argued, their interaction with the system which decides what their application will be and therefore what 'all or nothing' is to mean as a characteristic of rules. The above is not Dworkin's idea of how rules of recognition work. He believes that for a rule of recognition to be applicable it must be *justificatory*. He says that 'we could not devise any formula for *testing* how much and what kind of institutional support is necessary to make a principle a legal principle. . .'. But if he had understood that the point of the 'formula' or rule of recognition is not to provide 'support' but (only) to provide public, clear and dateable evidence that a proposition is a legal proposition, he would not have attacked the positivist on this point.

Of course, rules of recognition do not tell us how to construe the law. That problem is unavoidable and persists on any view of these matters. The problem which Dworkin has confused with the function of rules of recognition concerns which propositions *should be* allowed entry to the legal system. That, however, is the problem of how the system as a whole works and not of how one small part does. But the magnitude and importance of this concern should not make us overlook the existence of other concerns of the system and the devices which have evolved to deal with them.

All of our rule-governed practices have meta-rules which contain information about how we are to know whether or not a particular proposition or act is officially confirmed as part of a practice and when it becomes so. This has been called 'a rule of recognition'[3] or 'a constitutive feature'[4] or 'an invoking rule'.[5] For a narrower range of practices it has been called a 'performatory utterance'[6] where, according to the meta-rule, a (usually) verbal act itself is the event which is an invocation of a particular linguistic practice. The membership of this particular class of meta-rules is large. According to such rules, a judge's pronouncement under the correct conditions constitutes the sentencing of a defendant or a ruling on an objection; the Queen's signature on a document whose content has passed through other similar gates of formal acceptance means that this document (its contents) is now thereby the law of the land; each time a referee blows his whistle during a game we have an event which marks the fact that a certain decision has been taken by him or that some other game-related event, such as its end, has thereby occurred; if a proof in logic or mathematics accords with certain formal requirements – the axioms, the rules of inference and the syntax of well-formed formulae – then that constitutes its validity; if I say, 'I promise', ('warn,' 'marry,' 'commiserate') under certain conditions then that thereby constitutes the speaker's having performed such acts. When certain relations inhere among propositions, that constitutes justification, certain others constitute consistency, and others yet, truth.

In practices, then, for which fully responsible or standard action is required, rules of recognition will be essential since they supply one of the epistemic conditions without which such action cannot take place.

We saw in Chapter VII how the intention of an agent could be seen as the internal analogue of the proclamation of a law, serving to indicate what was to be done. An intention puts the act under a description, which is to put it under cognition, to make it therefore known to the agent himself, as it were. That is why when we are assured that an act is intentional and therefore known to the agent under a certain description, cognitive, we go on to infer responsibility. If we assume then that practices imply the occurrence of actions we may assume the need for rules of recognition at many levels. There will be such rules for what constitutes a promise, what constitutes an intentional act, what constitutes a certain utterance meaning this or that. This does not, however, give us licence to assume that the content of practices is totally determined by *such* rules of recognition. No practice commences without a great deal of content and form already at work and assumed. That content will be what is implied by agency and its ETP components. Any new content sanctioned by a rule of recognition will be subject to the considerations of the presuppositions. Justification of new content will then be a separate matter from its mere recognition as content, each governed by different rules. Its treatment as content will be subject to and determined by its justification. Enlightened, perhaps, by the knowledge that even justification is a practice governed by a rule of recognition which determines when we have it or what constitutes justification, a positivist may reformulate his position. He might now hold that a series of rules of recognition, which includes those of justification, fully determines the content of law. But this would not satisfy many positivists particularly those who have prized a simple, single and therefore, they believe, epistemically satisfactory rule which determines content. The trouble with this view has always been that content determined in this way may take us nowhere.

2

Let us now look at morality in the light of the above. If we look at the Ten Commandments, for example, a rule of recognition seems to have been satisfied at least in form. Those ten propositions were published, in stone as a matter of fact, as 'the word of God', so they were published under the right authority, if ever there was one.

There is something to be noticed here. When a moral edict is claimed to be the word of God or when the law of a state is given to us by a monarch's divine right, we find two functions fused. The first has to do solely with what is to count as a necessary and sufficient condition of a proposition being law (certain other things being in place, of course). This first function is concerned to produce clarity on that point alone. In our state, the parliament must duly pass a bill and the Queen's representative, the Governor General, must sign it. It is thereby law; that is what the rule of recognition for federal statutes requires in order to ensure definitive clarity on what is deemed law.

The second function is concerned with ensuring the right content of what is counted as law. It would be a comfort to know that a deity or monarch who gave his imprimatur to a law with the exercise of those first powers also had the quite different powers to ensure its wisdom. If he had the proper divine characteristics of omniscience and goodness, he would have the power to ensure that wisdom. To weld those two sets of powers together would ensure that no gap could exist between what is deemed law (by means of his first power) and what ought to become law (by means of the second).

Actually God embodied the virtues of the Perfect Agent. He

was, we know, omniscient, perfectly good and omnipotent. He therefore had all the requisite true beliefs, chose perfectly, that is always chose the right and the good and was an irresistible effector of his intentions. Naturally we should want to place in the hands of such an agent the authority to dictate the moral (and other) law. Hence a rule of recognition was needed, a sign of what the Word was. It is unfortunate that institutions today do not preserve that order of things: authority derived from desert. But we no longer believe that God, the Perfect Agent, is sufficiently present in either our monarchs or legislators, or even in His own right, to set us at ease regarding the question of how the deliberative powers of agency are being performed. And, although that belief was comforting and, therefore efficacious, it always contained a high degree of self-deception about how the process of the production of good laws actually worked.

Even the first function, for example, clarity about what conditions must be met for a law to be a law, is not to be found at work in morality today. In the past, we knew what the moral law was because we knew what His word was. It was found in the Ten Commandments and later, in the promulgations of the church. The divine right of the chief priest ruled in moral matters just as the divine right of the monarch ruled in political and legal matters. So, given a certain set of beliefs about God and His earthly surrogates, the rules of recognition worked well.

Morality has in the past (always) had rules of recognition which settled matters of its own content. Without such rules it would have foundered in just the ways which have been predicted of the law. It is therefore a critically unself-conscious argument of the sort we have seen made by Dworkin which holds that moral content, which requires rules of recognition for its own effective working, cannot in principle have rules of recognition which would govern its entry into the legal area. If the content of morality was, as it had to be, capable of being controlled by rules of recognition of its own, then that same content could be controlled by legal rules of recognition.

Now that we no longer believe that God's having so written on tablets or so spoken constitutes a certain set of moral rulings, we are apparently in a more puzzling position regarding morality than we are regarding legality. At least we know what sufficient and necessary conditions have to be satisfied for a law to be a law even though its wisdom is not guaranteed. But, we are apparently not in a position to say what conditions must be fulfilled to make a proposition a moral law. What is the moral law? And by what authority?

Custom might be suggested as the authority. The rule might be that what is customary, say in certain sexual matters, determines what is moral or immoral. We could be reasonably clear about what is customary and therefore reasonably clear about what to recognize as moral or immoral. Customs can have the disadvantage of being mixed or unclear when our attitudes are in flux or mixed. This might be thought to have the advantage of honesty, which we might prize over clarity, in that the rules being created by mixing or changing custom would reflect more faithfully our actual attitudes on these matters. However, this will not do since it would permit contradictory moral laws – a consequence of which would be to lose even the effects of honesty.

Furthermore, what would we do in the hard moral case where, *ex hypothesi*, custom cannot inform us? One could in defence say that a custom could exist whereby a referee decides what is binding in a hard case: we could, that, is, have a customary way of deciding these cases which cannot be decided by custom. That could work but it would not then be a system run exclusively on custom. Rather, for these crucial sorts of cases, it has one key custom, which is to decide by means other than custom. So custom or precedent counts where it works, and an arbitrator's decision counts where custom does not work. The church probably acted in this way on moral interstices as they arose, and some claim that law works that way as well. But morality does not now work that way except for those who subscribe to the present existence, authority and power of moral referees.

Another possible suggestion is that a set of basics have gained *de facto* acceptance and that beyond that certain rules of inference operate whereby further valid moral laws are obtained. Mathematics proceeds in this way; the validity of a proposition is recognized if it is derivable according to certain rules of inference. So the rules of inference are the rules of recognition of logical validity. Similarly, we might say the rules of moral inference, such as (for example) some form of utility-calculus, are the rules whereby we recognize the legitimate extension of the basic agreed list of moral propositions.

This might work (certainly utilitarians think it works); but the idea that a rule of inference acts as a rule of recognition is not, at present, a sufficiently clear part of our moral affairs, as shown by the fact that there are theoreticians and laymen who hold that certain (many) moral propositions are impervious in their rectitude, whatever their consequences may be. What this shows us is that we do not at present have (institutional) moral devices which allow us to settle the hard moral case. From a 'moral point of view', morality is not better off than legality once we move away from clear cases. Actually, having lost its latent institutional superstructure, morality is worse off than legality so long as they agree on the initially clear cases.

Suppose we admit that there is no rule of recognition whose satisfaction would allow us to answer the question of 'What is the moral law?' and 'By whose authority?' with the required certainty. In that case we are left with the following as descriptive of morality:

(1) a set of *desiderata*,
(2) their generally agreed ordering for simple cases,
(3) certain standard rules of inference and some of scope, such as universalizability,
(4) a means of discovering the further ordering relationships among these *desiderata* through a study of their consequences for each other, and finally,
(5) a means of increasing this web of *desiderata* from the basic set to include those which are derivative but necessary or sufficient for the first.

From these types of constituents, moral rules or theorems will be formulated. We can assume that we know some of the *desiderata*: freedom, dignity, safety, privacy, property, honesty, kindness, sympathy and so on. We also probably know a good deal about the ordering of these *desiderata*, *ceteris paribus*. If nothing else is at stake we would probably prefer freedom to either sympathy or kindness; safety to privacy or property; truth to reputation. But this is not much to know. The moment things become slightly complicated, we find ourselves hampered by the particular case and are unable to see the general principles at work. Our body of moral theory and moral knowledge is very thin. It is, although powerful, a very small body of logically early doctrine with very little worked out and agreed beyond that. Once we have a well-developed set of rules which we have derived by logical inference from a set of basic moral propositions, such as the moral law found in the *Mishna*, then we have something like a legal system. If the sort of thing the *Mishna* represents has continued to exist and grow then it is in the law proper that it is to be found.

It may well be that a well-functioning set of moral beliefs, or morality, can function only if housed in either a legal system or religion or something similar. Both Bentham and Hobbes saw this. Bentham saw morality housed in either the science of utilitarianism, or, what he thought was equivalent, a legal order.

How does this leave the question of how the law is to be judged morally? It is unavoidable for law to incorporate our 'moral principles'. How could we rationally allow the construction and continuance of a machine which has the impact and the power of law unless we were guaranteed through its structure those considerations we call 'moral'? Whatever else the concept of morality harbours, it implies *desiderata* and goals we must value. That is its superlative attraction and force. Law must at least be in accord with those goals if this part of life is governed by reason at all. Actually, law is more than merely consistent with these goals; it subsumes all of them: we cannot cite a decisively moral principle which is not also a legal one. Just as science must incorporate an empiricism, just as physics must be *natural* physics, so law must incorporate a morality: all law must be 'natural' law. And we must be allowed to say one final time that this 'natural' content begins with agency. To this extent there is an identity between law and morals.

Law then commences with moral goals already internalized. But once this moral beginning is subsumed, there is no *ex cathedra*, no external, 'moral' argument which is not already a fully legal argument. There will exist no external set of moral benchmarks by which law is measurable any more than there exists for morality an external measure of itself. The law may be measured against its own canons such as consistency and the presence of certain ('moral') assumptions. But then if Bentham asks, 'What do we choose, the law as it is or the law as it ought to be?', the correct reply is always, 'The law as it ought to be.' From that point on, however, from the point beyond the initial subsumption into legality of moral principles, the question of what the law ought to be will be an internal legal question. Legality is the science of morality, the science, that is, of an initial set of propositions, the science of an initially small and simple body of 'knowledge'. But eventually even this original body of moral data injected at the commencement of the legal science will be amendable in both content and order and size by considerations which are brought out as the body of legal knowledge develops. At this point if Bentham were to ask, 'What do we choose, the law as it is or as it ought to be'?, our answer must be, 'Only the law knows what ought to be.'

NOTES

I THE CONCEPT OF ACTION

1 For an account of epistemological adjusters and their implications see S. Coval and D.D. Todd, 'Adjusters and sense data', *American Philosophical Quarterly*, 1972, vol. 9, pp. 107-12.
2 See J.L. Austin, 'A plea for excuses', *Proceedings of the Aristotelian Society', 1956-7, vol. 57, pp. 1-29.*
3 [1891] 1 Q.B. 86.
4 These facts are based on a case reported in the Otago Daily Times, 30 April 1974, occurring in Christchurch, New Zealand.
5 *Vaughan* v. *Menlove* (1837) 3 Bing, N.C. 468; 132 E.R. 490.
6 *Palsgraf* v. *Long Island Railway Co.* (1928) 248 N.Y. 339; 162 N.E. 99.
7 It is reported by some of his students that J.L. Austin in his lectures on excuses in the late 1950s taught that only rather small movements were what we might call involuntary; she gave an involuntary gasp. We could, however, as easily entitle this section 'non-voluntariness' and leave it as it is. The important thing is whether such distinctions do exist. There very probably is a distinction between 'involuntary' and 'non-voluntary'. 'Involuntarily' might mean that 'the will' was not involved in the production of the action – the gasp slipped by it; and 'non-voluntarily' might mean that 'the will' was involved, but in conditions which prevented it from normal function.
8 *Gilbert* v. *Stone* (1648) Style 72; 82 E.R. 539 (K.B.).
9 *United States* v. *Holmes* (1842) Fed. Cas. No. 15383; C.C.E.D. Pa.
10 *Smith* v. *Stone* (1647) Style 65; 82 E.R. 533 (K.B.).
11 See Joel Feinberg's use of this phrase in 'Action and responsibility' in *Philosophy in America*, ed. Max Black, Ithaca, New York, Cornell University Press, 1965, pp. 134-60, and D. Davidson's criticism in 'Agency' in *Agent, Action and Reason*, ed. R. Binkley *et al.*,

Toronto, University of Toronto Press, 1971, pp. 3-26. See also: Donald Davidson, 'The logical form of action sentences', in N. Rescher, *The Logic of Decision and Action*, Pittsburgh, University of Pittsburgh Press, 1966, pp. 81-120; 'Causal relations', *Journal of Philosophy*, 1967, vol. 64, pp. 691-703; 'The individuation of events', *Inquiry*, 1970, vol. 13, pp. 140-8.

II ACTIONS AND DEFENCES

1 Some defences are not action-related and thus not susceptible to a standard action theory analysis. These include lawful authority, pardon, and double jeopardy.
2 *Our Criminal Law* (1976) Law Reform Commission of Canada Report, at p. 23.
3 (1843) 10 Cl. and F. 200 (H.L.) at p. 210.
4 *Falkenham* v. *Zwicker* (1978) 93 D.L.R. (3d) 289.
5 S.C. Coval, J.C. Smith and J. Rush, 'Out of the maze: towards a clear understanding of the test for remoteness of damages in negligence', *Canadian Bar Review*, 1983, vol. 61, pp. 559-94.
6 Glanville Williams, *The Mental Element in Crime*, Jerusalem, Magnes Press, Hebrew University, 1965.
7 See the protracted discussion of this distinction in the case of *D.P.P.* v. *Hyam* [1975] A.C. 55 (H.L.), particularly the judgment of Lord Hailsham.
8 Glanville Williams, *op. cit.*, note 6, at pp. 30-2.
9 This category is described in a way dictated by the decision of the Supreme Court of Canada in *R.* v. *City of Sault Ste Marie* (1978) 40 C.C.C. (2d) 353 where a clear distinction is drawn between strict liability offences and offences of absolute liability. In England no such distinction is made by the courts.

III AGENTS AND RIGHTS

1 Some examples of various forms of this view are to be found in H.J. McCloskey, 'Rights', *Philosophical Quarterly*, 1965, vol. 15, pp. 115-27; A.I. Melden, *Rights and Persons*, Berkeley and Los Angeles, University of California Press, 1977, at pp. 10, 57; D.D. Raphael, 'Human rights', *Proceedings of the Aristotelian Society*, 1965, suppl. vol. 39, pp. 205-36, at pp. 210-11; J. Feinberg, 'Wasserstrom on human rights', *Journal of Philosophy*, 1964, vol. 61, pp. 641-5, and 'Duties, rights, and claims', *American Philosophical Quarterly*, 1966, vol. 3, pp. 137-44, at p. 142; M.P. Golding, 'Towards a theory of human rights', *Monist*, 1968, vol. 52, pp. 530-2; H.D. Aiken, 'Rights, human and otherwise', *Monist*, 1968, vol. 52, p. 503.
2 See Ronald Dworkin's view in *Taking Rights Seriously*, Cambridge,

Mass., Harvard University Press, 1977, at p. 82 and Ch. 6 for examples.

3 Alan Gewirth, in his book *Reason and Morality*, Chicago, University of Chicago Press, 1978, expresses the idea that the concept of action provides the basis for a 'logical derivation of a supreme substantive moral principle'. He also believes that 'purposiveness and voluntarism exhaust the generic features of action', and his arguments of justification tend to remain at the generic level. Our enterprise is not unlike his in spirit but we emphasize considerably more the analysis of action which results in a highly articulated set of action-features. The members of this more particular set of features are therefore more perspicuously relatable to the basic evaluative judgments, or rights, which they subtend.

4 See John Locke, section 7, *Two Treatises of Government*, ed. Peter Laslett, Cambridge, Cambridge University Press, 1967.

IV THE POSITIVIST'S FEAR

1 Wilfred Sellars, 'Empiricism and the philosophy of mind', *Minnesota Studies in the Philosophy of Science*, vol. 1, Minneapolis, University of Minnesota Press, 1958, pp. 293-305.

2 Donald Davidson, 'Actions, reasons, and causes', *Journal of Philosophy*, 1963, vol. 60, pp. 685-700.

3 See *Liberalism and the Limits of Justice* by Michael Sandel, Cambridge, Cambridge University Press, 1982, and 'The procedural republic and the unencumbered self', in *Political Theory*, 1981, vol. 12, pp.81-96, also by Sandel.

4 H.L.A.Hart, 'Positivism and the separation of law and morals', *Harvard Law Review*, 1957-8, vol. 71, pp. 593-629; L. Fuller, 'Positivism and fidelity to law – a reply to Professor Hart', *Harvard Law Review*, 1957-8, vol. 71, pp. 630-72. Other legal theorists have taken the debate further. See for example, R.M. Dworkin, *Taking Rights Seriously* Cambridge, Mass., Harvard University Press, 1977, Ch. 2, p. 14; G. Hughes, 'Rules, policy and decision making', *Yale Law Journal*, 1967-8, vol. 77, pp. 411-39; J. Raz, 'Legal principles and the limits of the law', *Yale Law Journal*, 1971-2, vol. 81, pp. 823-54.

5 *Supra*, note 1.

6 *Supra*. note 1.

7 See for example 'Legal education and public policy: professional training in the public interest', *Yale Law Journal*, 1942-3, vol. 52, pp. 203-95, at p. 242. The statement 'a contextually oriented jurisprudence is a built-in device for maintaining the ever-precarious balance between rigidifying tendencies and the openness of mind required to keep in contact with the stream of new emergents in the life of society', 'Jurisprudence in policy-oriented perspective', *University of*

Florida Law Review, 1966-7, vol. 19, pp. 486-513, at p. 500 reflects the disjunction which McDougal and Lasswell see between stability and teleological change.

8 See John Rawls, 'Two concepts of rules', *Philosophical Review*, 1955, vol. 64, pp. 3-32; D. Lyons, *Forms and Limits of Utilitarianism*, Oxford, Clarendon Press, 1965; J.C. Smart, 'Extreme and restricted utilitarianism', *Philosophical Quarterly*, 1956, vol. 6, pp. 344-54.

9 There was actually such a case. The case of the 'red-neck' Sheriff and the death-bed promise are other examples of the same form.

10 H.L.A. Hart calls this feature the recognition feature of the law; J.L. Austin has been taken wrongly to have held that acts such as promising were constituted entirely by a 'performatory' act, that is, constituted entirely by their invoking feature; hence, mistaken talk as in J.R. Searle's *Speech Acts*, London, Cambridge University Press, 1969, of an act as being constitutive of some larger act. We think it better to speak of certain acts as being the invocation of a practice or some larger act since it displays more clearly its role within the full setting of the practice. See also J. Raz, *Practical Reason and Norms*, London, Hutchinson, 1975, at p. 49.

11 Lewis Carroll, *Through the Looking-Glass*, 'When I use a word,' Humpty Dumpty said, in a rather scornful tone, 'it means just what I choose it to mean – neither more nor less.'

12 J.L. Austin, *How to do Things with Words*, Cambridge, Mass., Harvard University Press, 1962.

13 In Paul Grice's etymon article, 'Meaning', *Philosophical Review*, 1957, vol. 66. pp. 377-88, the seeds of a causal theory of meaning were firmly planted. Since then the evidence has grown that meaning is actually to be so analysed. Stephen Schiffer's recent book, *Meaning*, Oxford, Clarendon Press, 1972, would take one through the subtleties of the theory as it stands closer to today and also through some of the relevant literature since Grice's first piece.

V RULES AND *CETERIS PARIBUS*

1 Criminal Code, R.S.C. 1970, Ch. C-34, ss. 12 and 13. At common law there is an irrebuttable presumption that children under a certain age (the age has fluctuated) cannot commit a crime. Above this age, and up to a further age limit, the presumption may be rebutted by showing that the child had the requisite mental capacity. Children are not liable for intentional torts unless they understand the nature of their actions: *Tillander* v. *Gosselin* (1966) 60 D.L.R. (2d) 18. Nor are they liable in negligence unless they are old enough to realize the nature of the risk which they create, *Walmsley* v. *Humenick* [1954] 2 D.L.R. 232; *McHale* v. *Watson* (1966) 115 C.L.R. 199.

2 The Criminal Code, R.S.C. 1970, Ch. C-34, s.16; J.C. Smith and B. Hogan, *Criminal Law* (3rd edn), London, Butterworths, 1970, at p.

130; and G. Williams, *Criminal Law* (2nd edn), London, Stevens, 1961, at p. 428. For civil liability in regard to intentional torts see *Morriss* v. *Marsden* [1952] 1 All E.R. 925 (Q.B.); *Phillips* v. *Soloway* (1956) 6 D.L.R. (2d) 570 (Man. Q.B.); *McGuire* v. *Almy* (1937) 8 N.E. (2d) 760 (Mass.). See *Buckley* v. *Smith Transport* [1946] 4 D.L.R. 721 (O.C.A.); and *Slattery* v. *Haley* [1923] 3 D.L.R. 156 (O.C.A.) regarding negligence and insanity.

3 *The Queen* v. *Cottle* [1958] N.Z.L.R. 999; *R.* v. *Charlson* [1955] 1 All E.R. 859 (C.A.); *Bratty* v. *A.-G. for Northern Ireland* [1963] A.C. 386 (H.L.). Where automatism intersects with insanity it is treated as a defence of insanity; where it intersects with intoxication it is the defence of intoxication. Only where it is caused by neither of these does it lie as a separate defence and grant a complete acquittal. *R.* v. *Hartridge* (1966) 57 D.L.R. (2d) 332 (Sask. C.A.).

4 *D.P.P. for Northern Ireland* v. *Lynch* [1975] A.C. 653 (H.L.); *Abbott* v. *The Queen* [1976] 3 W.L.R. 462 (P.C.); *Subramaniam* v. *Public Prosecutor* [1956] 1 W.L.R. 965 (P.C.). The Criminal Code, R.S.C. 1970, Ch. C-34, s.17; Smith and Hogan, *supra*, note 2 at pp. 751-69.

5 *Beaver* v. *R* [1957] S.C.R. 531 (Canadian position).

6 Smith and Hogan, *supra*, note 2 at pp. 148-54 (English position).

7 In the law of torts a mistake of fact can negate intent, and if the mistake is a reasonable one, there would be no basis for liability in negligence.

8 *The Queen* v. *Tolson* (1889) 23 Q.B.D. 168. In Canada see s.254 (2)(a) of the Criminal Code where the same rule applies as an exception to the general proposition that only an honest belief is required.

9 A.G. Guest, *Anson's Law of Contract* (24th edn), Oxford, Clarendon Press, 1975, at p. 476; G.C. Cheshire, C.H.S. Fifoot and M.P. Furmston, *Law of Contract* (10th edn), London, Butterworths, 1981, at p. 512.

10 *Maritime National Fish, Ltd.* v. *Ocean Trawlers, Ltd.* [1935] A.C. 524 (P.C.). *Denmark Productions, Ltd.* v. *Boscobel Productions, Ltd.* [1968] 3 W.L.R. 841 (C.A.).

11 *Supra*, note 2 at pp. 746-7. See also *The Queen* v. *Bamber*, 5 Q.B. 279, 114 E.R. 1254, *Hardcastle* v. *Bielby* [1892] 1 Q.B. 709. *Model Penal Code*, s.201 (1) (Proposed Official Draft, 1962).

12 *Lim Chin Aik* v. *The Queen* [1963] A.C. 160, 174-5 (P.C.).

13 Negligent mistake of fact is not a defence in England. *R.* v. *King* [1963] 3 All E.R. 561 (C.A.). *R.* v. *Gould* [1968] 2 Q.B. 65 (C.A.), although it *may* be in Canada. *Beaver* v. *R.*, *supra*, note 5.

14 *Director of Public Prosecutions* v. *Beard* [1920] A.C. 479 (H.L.), *D.P.P.* v. *Majewski* [1975] 2 W.L.R. 623 (H.L.), Smith and Hogan, *supra*, note 2 at pp. 151-7.

15 See Chapter II.

16 We recognize that there is conflicting authority on the question of

whether mistake renders a contract void or merely voidable. One line of traditional authorities supports the proposition that a contract violated by mistake is void, but modern authority tends towards a theory of voidability.

17 *Holder* v. *Holder* [1968] 1 All E.R. 665 (C.A.), at p. 672.

18 This is known as the 'but for' test. For a detailed analysis see H.L.A. Hart and A.M. Honore, *Causation in the Law*, Oxford, Clarendon Press, 1959, Ch. 5.

19 *McWilliams* v. *Sir William Arrol and Co., Ltd.* [1962] 1 W.L.R. 295 (H.L.).

20 Historically three principle rules of statutory interpretation have developed, the Mischief Rule or the Rule in *Heydon's Case* (1584) 3 Co. Rep. 7a, 76 E.R. 637, the Literal or Plain Meaning Rule, or the Rule in the *Sussex Peerage Case* (1844) 11 C1. and F. 85, 8 E.R. 1034, and the Golden Rule, or the Rule in *Grey* v. *Pearson* (1857) 6 H.L.C. 61, 10 E.R. 1216. The Literal Meaning Rule was enunciated to prevent what were considered to be excessive judicial modifications of statutes under the Mischief Rule, and the Golden Rule was developed to escape the restraints of the Literal Meaning Rule. The Mischief and Golden Rules require statutes to be interpreted according to their objectives, and the Literal Meaning Rule places restraints on this exercise.

21 *Abbot* v. *Middleton* (1858) 7 H.L.C. 67, at 114, 11 E.R. 28, at 46. *Mitchell* v. *Torup* (1766) Parker 227, 233, 145 E.R. 764, 766. *River Wear Commissioners* v. *Adamson* (1877) 2 A.C. 743 (H.L.), at 764-5. *Victoria City* v. *Bishop of Vancouver Island* [1921] 2 A.C. 384 (J.C.P.C.), at 387.

22 E.A. Driedger, in *The Construction of Statutes*, Toronto, Butterworths, 1983, at p. 87 states, 'Today there is only one principle or approach, namely, the words of an Act are to be read in their entire context in their grammatical and ordinary sense harmoniously with the scheme of the Act, the object of the Act and the intention of Parliament.'

23 S. 11, Interpretation Act, R.S.C. 1970, c. I-23.

24 *Tedla* v. *Ellman* (1939) 19 N.E. (2d) 987, 280 N.Y. 124.

25 *Ibid.*, at p. 991.

26 See *Kitson* (1955) 39 C.A.R. 66 for an example of where the defence of necessity was neither raised nor applied. The court appeared to reach the ridiculous conclusion that it is better to risk one's life rather than to stop a car when one is impaired, and thus break the law.

27 Williams, *supra*, note 2 at pp. 722 and 731.

28 S. 3.02 (Proposed Official Draft, 1962).

29 'The defence of necessity', *Current Legal Problems*, 1953, vol. 6, pp. 216-35.

30 (1801) 3 C. Rob. 240 at 266, 165 E.R. 450 at 459.

31 *Supra*, note 29 at p. 224.

32 One is not liable in torts for causing damage to property in order to

preserve life. See *Manor and Co. Ltd.* v. *M.V. 'Sir John Crosbie'* (1966) 52 D.L.R. (2d) 48 (Exch. Ct.). (Where the risk is only to property and not to lives, the loss may be treated differently. See *Vincent* v. *Lake Erie Transportation Co.* (1910) 124 N.W. 221.) Since the civil side of the law justifies the destruction of property to save lives, it cannot be considered even to be a civil wrong to do so.

33 *Riggs* v. *Palmer* (1889) 115 N.Y. 506; 22 N.E. 188 (N.Y.C.A.).

34 G. Hughes, 'Rules, policy and decision making', *Yale Law Journal*, 1967-8, vol. 77, pp. 411-39; R.M. Dworkin, *Taking Rights Seriously*, Cambridge, Mass., Harvard University Press, 1977, Ch. 2, p. 14.

35 *Yale Law Journal*, 1971-2, vol. 81, pp. 823-54.

VI THE ANTI-POSITIVIST'S FEAR

1 R.M. Dworkin, *Taking Rights Seriously*, Cambridge, Mass., Harvard University Press, 1977, at.p. 14.

2 (1889) 115 N.Y. 506, 22 N.E. 188.

3 *Supra*, note 1 at p. 25.

4 *Ibid.*

5 *Ibid.*

6 *Amicable Society* v. *Bolland* (1830) 4 Bligh (N.S.) 194 at 211; 5 E.R. 70 at 76.

7 *In the Estate of Cunigunda (otherwise Cora) Crippen, decd.* [1911] P. 108; *Re Johnson* [1950] 2 D.L.R. 69 (Man. Q.B.).

8 *Mutual Life Insurance Company of New York* v. *Armstrong* (1886) 117 U.S. 997.

9 [1892] 1 Q.B. 147. If the object to be ensured by public policy in this case was that such crimes be not motivated by the law itself, as it were, then it is not clear that allowing the children to take under the will would not constitute such a motivation for the mother. The court in the *Cleaver* case would appear to disagree with the court in *Fauntleroy's* case over what constitutes a motivation or a 'lack of restraint' in such matters.

10 *Ibid.*, p. 156.

11 *Ibid.*, p. 155.

12 *In the Estate of Hall, Hall* v. *Knight and Baxter* [1914] P.1; *Lundy* v. *Lundy* (1895) 24 S.C.R. 650.

13 *Re Callaway (decd.), Callaway* v. *Treasury Solicitor* [1956] Ch. 559.

14 *Schobelt* v. *Barber* (1967) 60 D.L.R. (2d) 519; *Bierbrauer* v. *Moran* (1935) 279 N.Y.S. 176.

15 *Re Callaway, supra*, n. 13, *Re Johnson, supra*, n. 7.

16 *Beresford* v. *Royal Insurance Co. Ltd.* [1938] A.C. 586 (H.L.).

17 I.D. Browne, *MacGillivray on Insurance Law* (5th edn), London, Sweet & Maxwell, 1961, at p. 253.

18 *Askey* v. *Golden Wine Co. Ltd* [1948] 2 All E.R. 35 (K.B.); *Haseldine* v. *Hosken* [1933] 1 K.B. 822.

19 *Strand Electric and Engineering Co. Ltd* v. *Brisford Entertainments Ltd*. [1952] 2 Q.B. 246.
20 *Olwell* v. *Nye & Nissen Co.* (1946) 169 A.L.R. 139.
21 *Wasson* v. *California Standard Co.* (1965) 47 D.L.R. (2d) 71; *Pretu* v. *Donald Tidey Co. Ltd.* (1965) 53 D.L.R. (2d) 504.
22 *Cassell & Co. Ltd* v. *Broome* [1972] A.C. 1027 (H.L.).
23 *In re Houghton* [1915] 2 Ch. 173; *Braumann* v. *Nordstrom* (1961) 37 W.W.R. 16 (S.C.C.).
24 *Tinline* v. *White Cross Insurance Association, Ltd.* [1921] 3 K.B. 327; *James* v. *British General Insurance Co. Ltd.* [1927] 2 K.B. 311; *Bunting* v. *Hartford Accident and Indemnity Co. and Hartford Fire Insurance Co.* [1955] 2 D.L.R. 700; *Messersmith* v. *American Fidelity Co.* (1921) 133 N.E. 432; *New Amsterdam Casualty Co.* v. *Jones* (1943) 135 F.(2d) 191.
25 *O'Hearn* v. *Yorkshire Insurance Co.* (1921) 50 *Ont. L.R.* 377. Early decisions such as this one are considered to be wrongly decided and have not been followed.
26 *Re Giles* [1971] 3 W.L.R. 640 (Ch. D.).
27 [1970] 2 Q.B. 626 at p. 640; on appeal [1971] 2 Q.B. 554.
28 (1857) 6 H.L.C. 443 at 461; 10 E.R. 1368 at 1375.
29 *Ibid.*
30 (1890) 45 Ch. D. 430 at 438.
31 (1894) 63 F. 310 at 317.
32 Courts have held a breach of contract to be an illegal act. *Ahmed Angullia Bin Hadjee Mohamed Sallah Angullia* v. *Estate and Trust Agencies Ltd* [1938] A.C. 624 (J.C.P.C.); *Rookes* v. *Barnard* [1964] A.C. 1129 (H.L.). It does not follow from this, however, that it is a wrong as defined according to the teleology of the rule in question.
33 Law Reform Committee, 14th Report, *Acquisition of Easements and Profits by Prescription*, para. 8 (London, HMSO, 1966).
34 (1834) 1 C.M. and R. 211 at p. 219; 149 E.R. 1057 at p. 1060.
35 *Union Central Life Ins. Co.* v. *Elizabeth Trust Co.* (1936) 183 A. 181 at 185. See also *Re Gore* (1972) 23 D.L.R. (3d) 534.
36 A strict positivist, in so far as he is limited to the first-order rules themselves in his description of 'the law', thus cannot even find that there is a conflict.
37 (1960) 32 N.J. 358; 161 A. (2d) 69.
38 Dworkin, *supra*, note 1 at p. 24.
39 *Henningsen* v. *Bloomfield Motors, Inc.* (1960) 161 A. (2d) 69 at 95.
40 *Lowe* v. *Peers (1768) 4 Burr. 2225 at 2233; 98 E.R. 160 at 164.*
41 *Collins* v. *Blantern* (1767) 2 Wils. K.B. 347 at 348; 95 E.R. 850 at 851.
42 For examples, of the many cases which can be cited to illustrate each of the various kinds of contracts or contractual provisions which are void on grounds of public policy, see G.C. Cheshire and C.H.S. Fifoot, *The Law of Contract* (10th edn), London, Butterworths, 1981, at pp. 308-78.

43 This formulation tends to oversimplify the common law relating to this subject as it fails to draw a distinction between 'illegal contracts' which are void and consequently not enforceable, and contracts which are void only in so far as they contravene public policy and are therefore enforceable in part. To accurately reflect the state of the common law we would need to draft at least two second-order rules.
44 (1889) 22 N.E. 188 at 189.
45 *Ibid.*, p. 190.
46 [1947] 4 D.L.R. 393.
47 *Ibid.*, p. 395.
48 Dworkin, *supra*, note 1 at p. 39. We shall deal more comprehensively with the question of whether principles may have rules of recognition in Chapter VIII.
49 H.C. Gutteridge, 'Abuse of rights', *Cambridge Law Journal*, 1933-5, vol. 5, pp. 22-45. We are most grateful to Professor Otto Kahn-Freund who drew the principle of abuse of right and the above article to our attention.
50 German Civil Code (Art. 226). See Gutteridge, *op. cit.*, p. 36.
51 Swiss Civil Code (Art. 2). See Gutteridge, *op. cit.*, p. 39.
52 Trib. Civ. Compiegne, *Dalloz Periodique*, 1913 2. 177; Ariens et Re. *Dalloz Periodique*, 1917 1.79. See Gutteridge, *op. cit.*, p. 33.
53 [1895] A.C. 587.

VII THE METAPHYSICS OF LAW

1 See Donald Davidson, 'Causal relations', Essay 7 in *Essays on Actions and Events*, Oxford, Oxford University Press, 1982; and 'The individuation of events', *Essays in Honor of Carl Hempel*, ed. N. Rescher, Dordrecht, Holland, D. Reidel, 1969, pp. 216-34; and 'Events as particulars', *Nous*, vol. 4, 1970.
2 *Dwyer* v. *Staunton* [1947] D.L.R. 393.
3 J.C. Smith, 'The processes of adjudication and regulation, a comparison', Ch. 3 in *Rights and Regulations: Ethical, Political, and Economic Issues*, ed. J.R. Machan and B. Johnson, Cambridge, Mass., Ballinger, 1983 at p. 71.
4 See Hillary Putnam, 'The meaning of meaning', in *Philosophical Papers Vol. 2: Mind, Language and Reality*, Cambridge, Cambridge University Press, 1974, pp. 215-71; also Saul Kripke, 'Naming and necessity', in *Semantics of Natural Language*, ed. G. Harman and D. Davidson, Dordrecht, Holland, D. Reidel, 1972, at p. 304.
5 See, for example, Paul Churchland, *Scientific Realism and the Plasticity of Mind*, Cambridge, Cambridge University Press, 1979, especially the introduction.
6 See J.C. Smith, *Liability in Negligence*, London, Sweet & Maxwell, 1984, p. 29.
7 [1932] A.C. 562 (H.L.).

8 *Supra*, note 6 at pp. 15-19.
9 Per Lord Wilberforce in *Anns, Merton London Borough Council* [1978] A.C. 728 at 751-2 (H.L.).
10 *Supra*, note 6 at pp. 75-89.

VIII THE AUTONOMY OF LAW

1 H.L.A.Hart, 'Positivism and the separation of law and morals', *Harvard Law Review*, 1957-8, vol. 71, pp. 593-629, at p. 614.
2 R.W. Dworkin, *Taking Rights Seriously*, Cambridge, Mass., Harvard University Press, 1977, at p. 40.
3 H.L.A. Hart, *The Concept of Law*, Oxford, Clarendon Press, 1961, at p. 92.
4 J.R. Searle, *Speech Acts*, London, Cambridge University Press, 1969, at p. 33.
5 S.C. Coval and J.C. Smith, 'The causal theory of law', *Cambridge Law Journal*, 1977, vol. 36, pp. 110-51, at pp. 116-17.
6 J.L.Austin, *How To Do Things With Words*, Cambridge, Mass., Harvard University Press, 1962, Lecture I.

CASE INDEX

NAME INDEX

SUBJECT INDEX

International Library of Philosophy

Editor: Ted Honderich

(Demy 8vo)

Allen, R.E. and Furley, David J. (eds.), **Studies in Presocratic Philosophy**
Vol. 1: The Beginnings of Philosophy *326 pp. 1970.*
Vol. 2: Eleatics and Pluralists *448 pp. 1975.*
Armstrong, D.M., **Perception and the Physical World** *208 pp. 1961.* **A Materialist Theory of the Mind** *376 pp. 1967.*
Bambrough, Renford (Ed.), **New Essays on Plato and Aristotle** *184 pp. 1965.*
Barry, Brian, **Political Argument** *382 pp. 1965.*
Becker, Lawrence C. **On Justifying Moral Judgments 212 pp. 1973.**
† Benenson, F.C., **Probability, Objectivity and Evidence** *224 pp. 1984.*
†* Blum, Lawrence, **Friendship, Altruism and Morality** *256 pp. 1980.*
Brentano, Franz, **The Foundation and Construction of Ethics** *398 pp. 1973.*
The Origin of our Knowledge of Right and Wrong *184 pp. 1969.*
Psychology from an Empirical Standpoint *436 pp. 1973.*
Sensory and Noetic Consciousness *168 pp. 1981.*
† Budd, M., **Music and the Emotions** *208 pp. 1985.*
† Clarke, D.S., **Practical Inferences** *160 pp. 1985.*
Crombie, I.M., **An Examination of Plato's Doctrine**
Vol. 1: Plato on Man and Society *408 pp. 1962.*
Vol. 2: Plato on Knowledge and Reality *584 pp. 1963.*
† Davies, Martin, **Meaning, Quantification, Necessity** *294 pp. 1981.*
Dennett, D.C., **Content and Conciousness** *202 pp. 1969.*
Detmold, M.J., **The Unity of Law and Morality** *288 pp. 1984.*
Ducasse, C.J., **Truth, Knowledge and Causation** *264 pp. 1969.*
Fann, K.T. (Ed.), **Symposium on J.L. Austin** *512 pp. 1969.*
Findlay, J.N., **Plato: The Written and Unwritten Doctrines** *498 pp. 1974.*
† Findlay, J.N., **Wittgenstein: A Critique** *240 pp. 1984.*
Flew, Anthony, **Hume's Philosophy of Belief** *296 pp. 1961.*
† Fogelin, Robert J., **Hume's skepticism in the Treatise of Human Nature** *192 pp. 1985.*
† Foster, John, **The Case for Idealism** *280 pp. 1982.*
Goldman, Lucien, **The Hidden God** *424 pp. 1964.*
† Gray, John, **Mill on Liberty: A Defence** *160 pp. 1983.*
Holzman, Steven M. and Leich, Christopher H., **Wittgenstein: to Follow a Rule** *264 pp. 1981.*
† Honderich, Ted (Ed.), **Morality and Objectivity** *256 pp. 1985.*
†* Hornsby, Jennifer, **Actions** *152 pp. 1980.*
Husserl, Edmund, **Logical Investigations** *Vol. 1: 456 pp.*
Vol. 2: 464 pp. 1970.
* Linsky, Leonard, **Referring** *152 pp. 1967.*
Mackenzie, Brian D., **Behaviourism and the Limits of Scientific Method** *208 pp. 1977.*
†* Mackie, J.L., **Hume's Moral Theory** *176 pp. 1980.*